EAST OF EDEN

John Steinbeck

AUTHORED by Casey Diana
UPDATED AND REVISED by Jordan Berkow

COVER DESIGN by Table XI Partners LLC
COVER PHOTO by Olivia Verma and © 2005 GradeSaver, LLC

BOOK DESIGN by Table XI Partners LLC

Published by GradeSaver LLC, www.gradesaver.com

First published in the United States of America by GradeSaver LLC. 2006

ISBN 978–1–60259–067–0

Printed in the United States of America

For other products and additional information please visit
http://www.gradesaver.com

Table of Contents

Table of Contents

Biography of John Steinbeck (1902–1968)

John Steinbeck was born in Salinas, California in 1902, and spent most of his life in Monterey County, the setting of much of his fiction. He attended Stanford University intermittently between 1920 and 1926. Steinbeck did not graduate from Stanford, but instead chose to support himself through manual labor while writing. His experiences among the working classes in California lent authenticity to his depiction of the lives of the workers, who remain the central characters of his most important novels.

Steinbeck's first novel, *Cup of Gold*, was published in 1929, and was followed by *The Pastures of Heaven* and, in 1933, *To a God Unknown*. However, his first three novels were unsuccessful both critically and commercially. Steinbeck had his first success with *Tortilla Flat* (1935), an affectionate and gently humorous story about Mexican–Americans. Nevertheless, his subsequent novel, *In Dubious Battle* (1936) was notable for its markedly grim outlook. This novel is a classic account of a strike by agricultural laborers and the pair of Marxist labor organizers who engineer it, and is the first Steinbeck novel to encompass the striking social commentary that characterizes his most notable works. Steinbeck received even greater acclaim for the novella *Of Mice and Men* (1937), a tragic story about the strange, complex bond between two migrant laborers. His crowning achievement, *The Grapes of Wrath*, won Steinbeck a Pulitzer Prize and a National Book Award. It was also adapted into a classic film directed by John Ford that was named one of the American Film Institute's one hundred greatest films. The novel describes the migration of a dispossessed family from the Oklahoma Dust Bowl to California and critiques their subsequent exploitation by a ruthless system of agricultural economics.

After the best–selling success of *The Grapes of Wrath*, Steinbeck went to Mexico to collect marine life with the freelance biologist Edward F. Ricketts, and the two men collaborated on *Sea of Cortez* (1941), a study of the fauna of the Gulf of California. During World War II, Steinbeck wrote some effective pieces of government propaganda, among them *The Moon Is Down* (1942), a novel about Norwegians under the Nazis. He also served as a war correspondent. With the end of World War II and the move from the Great Depression to economic prosperity Steinbeck's work softened somewhat. While still containing the elements of social criticism that marked his earlier work, the three novels Steinbeck published immediately following the war, *Cannery Row* (1945), *The Pearl*, and *The Bus* (both 1947) were more sentimental and relaxed. Steinbeck also contributed to several screenplays. He wrote the original stories for several films, including *Lifeboat* (1944), directed by Alfred Hitchcock, and *A Medal for Benny*, and wrote the screenplay for Elia Kazan's *Viva Zapata!*, a biographical film about Emiliano Zapata, the Mexican peasant who rose to the presidency.

Steinbeck married Carol Henning in 1930 and lived with her in Pacific Grove, California. He spent much of his time in Monterey with his friend, Ricketts, at his Cannery Row laboratory, an experience which inspired his popular 1945 novel, *Cannery Row*. In 1943, Steinbeck married his second wife, Gwyndolyn Conger, with whom he had two children. 1948 was a particularly bad year for Steinbeck: Ricketts died, and Gwyndolyn left him. However, he found happiness in his 1950 marriage to Elaine Scott, with whom he lived in New York City. Two years later, he published the highly controversial *East of Eden*, the novel he called "the big one," set in the California Salinas Valley.

Steinbeck's later writings were comparatively slight works, but he did make several notable attempts to reassert his stature as a major novelist: *Burning Bright* (1950), *East of Eden* (1952), and *The Winter of Our Discontent* (1961). However, none of these works equaled the critical reputation of his earlier novels. Steinbeck's reputation is dependent primarily on the naturalistic, proletarian–themed novels that he wrote during the Depression. It is in these works that Steinbeck is most effective at building rich, symbolic structures and conveying the archetypal qualities of his characters. Steinbeck received the Nobel Prize for literature in 1962, and died in New York City in 1968.

About East of Eden

John Steinbeck published his highly controversial novel *East of Eden*, the work that he referred to as "the big one", in 1952. A symbolic recreation of the biblical story of Cain and Abel set in California's Salinas Valley, Steinbeck wrote the novel late in his life, in hopes of reclaiming his status as a major novelist. Described as Steinbeck's most ambitious novel, *East of Eden* centers on two families, the Trasks and the Hamiltons, both early inhabitants of California's Salinas Valley.

The author addressed the book to his sons, six year–old Thom and four year–old John, and positions himself as a minor character in the novel. Steinbeck wanted to record for his children the detailed, multi–faceted history of the Salinas Valley. In addition, the author considered the novel to be a "requiem for himself," and wrote, "it has everything in it I have been able to learn about my craft or profession in all these years." He also declared that "everything else I have written has been, in a sense, practice for this."

However, critics maintained that Steinbeck's expansive yet simplistic portrayal of good and evil and his overuse of biblical allusions overshadow the development of character and plot. *East of Eden* was not as well received as his earlier masterpieces. Indeed, the characters continue to be harshly criticized for being closer to symbols than actual people. In addition, the book continues to be critically disparaged because of its length and its overabundance of biblical references. *The New York Times* called *East of Eden* Steinbeck's "most problematic work."

Spanning the period between the American Civil War and World War I, the novel describes two generations of brothers. The first concerns the placid Adam Trask and his hot–tempered brother, Charles. Adam marries the evil Cathy Ames, who gives birth to twin sons, Aron and Cal, and abandons the family to return to prostitution. As the fair–haired, passive Aron and the dark–haired, energetic Cal grow, they vie for their father's affection. In a jealous frenzy, Cal tells Aron about his mother; Aron, in agony, joins the army and is killed. The unfortunate family is turned around, however, when Cal is offered surcease from his overwhelming guilt.

Despite harsh criticism, *East of Eden* became an instant best–seller and is considered by some to be one of Steinbeck's finest achievements. *East of Eden* remains Steinbeck's most controversial book – a disputed classic. The book was adapted as the 1955 film *East of Eden* by director Elia Kazan, starring James Dean and Julie Harris. The 1981 TV miniseries starred Timothy Bottoms and Jane Seymour. The novel recently saw a remarkable upsurge in popularity when television personality Oprah Winfrey selected *East of Eden* for her classics–only book club. Another film adaptation directed by Ron Howard is set to be released in 2006.

Ultimately, *East of Eden* deals with the cycle of sin, guilt, redemption, and freedom. Steinbeck's inspiration for the work can be found in the fourth chapter of Genesis, verses one through sixteen, which recounts the story of the biblical brothers Cain and Abel. The title is taken from Genesis 4:16.

Character List

Cathy Ames

The most evil character in the novel, Cathy (who is referred to as "Kate" in the second half of the novel) has no conscience whatsoever. A direct representation of Satan himself, Cathy lacks an essential human quality. After murdering her parents by setting fire to their home, she becomes a prostitute and the mistress of Mr. Edwards.

Adam Trask rescues Cathy when Edwards leaves her for dead, but after giving birth to twin sons, Cal and Aron, she shoots Adam when he attempts to stop her from leaving. She takes a job as a prostitute and poisons the brothel–owner, Faye, in an effort to take over the business. She gives her whores drugs, encourages sadomasochistic sexual practices, and blackmails her customers. Late in life, she commits suicide after meeting her son, Aron.

Abra Bacon

As a child Abra falls in love with young Aron Trask, but she later realizes that he is only in love with a glorified image of her. The daughter of a crooked Salinas politician, she wonders if a parent's evil can be inherited. However, she finds psychological surcease from Lee, whom she loves like a father.

Edwards

Edwards leads a double life: he runs a New England prostitution ring, but is married to a religious wife who believes that he runs a reputable business. He falls in love with Cathy after she approaches him for a job, but beats her severely and leaves her for dead after he finds out that she killed her parents.

Ethyl

Ethyl is a prostitute who sees Kate burying the empty poison bottles that she used to kill the brothel–owner, Faye. Her attempts to blackmail Kate fail.

Samuel Hamilton

The much–beloved Hamilton Family patriarch, Samuel Hamilton mentors and guides Adam Trask. He is contrasted with Cyrus, the dishonest Trask Family patriarch who commits the novel's original sin.

An Irish immigrant, Samuel demonstrates the positive principle of life. Although he farms the most barren land in the Salinas Valley, he educates himself, fathers nine children, and enjoys life until falling into despair after the death of Una, his favorite daughter.

Samuel Hamilton was, in fact, the name of John Steinbeck's grandfather. The character Samuel experiences initial distrust from his California neighbors, but over time becomes a highly respected and much appreciated member of the community. Although he never achieves material wealth, he is the happiest of all of the characters.

Dessie Hamilton

The most beloved daughter of Samuel and Liza Hamilton, Dessie opens a successful dressmaking business in Salinas, but falls in love with the wrong man and becomes depressed. Seriously ill, she is forced to close her shop and move back to the family ranch where her brother Tom inadvertently causes her death by giving her the wrong medicine.

Liza Hamilton

Samuel Hamilton's wise wife, and an excellent mother to the nine Hamilton children. Liza's no–nonsense attitude inspires her to work hard.

Olive Hamilton

A character based on the real–life mother of author John Steinbeck. The daughter of Samuel and Liza Hamilton, Olive becomes a schoolteacher and a loving mother.

Tom Hamilton

Samuel's depressed son and a poet, Tom can't seem to find his way in the world. Tom remains on the farm after his parents die and accidentally causes the death of his sister Dessie. He kills himself out of guilt.

Una Hamilton

The introspective daughter of Samuel and Liza Hamilton, Una marries a poor photographer and moves to Oregon, where she dies in poverty. Her death causes the beginning of Samuel's demise.

Will Hamilton

Samuel and Liza Hamilton's successful, level–headed son who succeeds in business, Will sells the first automobiles in the Salinas Valley and becomes Cal Trask's business–partner during the war.

Lee

The Chinese–American cook and housekeeper for the Trask family, Lee is forced to speak in the Chinese pidgin dialect that enables him to survive in America. An orphan, he raises Adam's children after they are abandoned by Cathy.

A scholar at heart, he remains a constant friend to Samuel Hamilton and Adam Trask, aiding them in their scholarly debates. He researches the Cain and Abel story and proffers the novel's central concept of "thou mayest."

Adam Trask

Adam Trask, one of the protagonists of *East of Eden*, is an honest man who transforms from a dreamy–eyed youth into a deeply caring father to Cal and Aron.

The son of Cyrus Trask, Adam falls in love with Cathy Ames when she wanders onto his farm. A representation of the biblical character Abel, who was stoned to death in a jealous rage by his brother Cain, his deathbed blessing of his son Cal validates *timshel*, a concept that denies the notion of predestination and authorizes free choice.

Alice Trask

The mother of Charles Trask, Alice treats Adam as her own son after his biological mother dies. She rarely talks, and smiles only when no one can see her. Adam presents her with little gifts, but she believes them to be from her own son, Charles.

Aron Trask

The son of Adam and Cathy Trask and the twin brother of Cal, Aron grows up to be deeply religious. He plans to enter the ministry in an attempt to escape the sinful world. He is Adam's favorite son and is in love with Abra Bacon. When his jealous brother Cal tells him that his mother is still alive and living as a prostitute, he joins the Army during World War I and dies in France soon after.

Cal Trask

The dark–haired son of Adam and Cathy, Cal (or Caleb) is deeply jealous of his seemingly perfect twin brother, Aron, and is the novel's second Cain figure. He indirectly kills his brother Aron by causing him to enlist in the Army. Ultimately, he represents the concept of timshel, the idea that people can overcome their backgrounds and choose to live free, moral lives.

Charles Trask

Charles' father, Cyrus Trask, favors his son Adam's gift of a puppy over Charles' gift of an expensive knife. In a jealous rage, Charles attempts to kill his brother. Charles represents the biblical character of Cain, who kills his brother when God favors Abel's lamb over his gift of grain. Charles remains on the family's Connecticut farm and amasses a fortune of $100,000 that he leaves to Adam and Cathy.

Cyrus Trask

Cyrus is the cruel and crooked father of Adam and Charles Trask, and the man who commits the "original sin" that inspires the action of the novel. He lies about his American Civil War record to garner himself an important job in Washington D.C. Crooked in his financial dealings, Cyrus leaves his sons an inheritance of $100,000.

Mrs. Trask

The religious mother of Adam Trask, Mrs. Trask commits suicide after her husband, Cyrus, returns from the Civil War with syphilis.

Joe Valery

An escaped convict, Joe works as Kate's bodyguard and bouncer and attempts to control her. Kate comes to rely on him until she realizes that he is extorting money from her. She commits suicide after informing the sheriff of his dark past.

Major Themes

The Land

Steinbeck utilizes the opening chapter's symbolic landscape to illustrate the overriding theme of good versus evil that permeates the novel: the Eden–like Salinas Valley is surrounded by the "good" sunlit Gabilan Mountains to the East, and the dark and foreboding "bad" Santa Lucias Mountains to the West. For most of the novel, the characters reside in this valley.

The land also reveals the characteristics of the two major families, the Hamilton and the Trasks. The Hamiltons settle in the driest land, but although their land is practically barren, they raise nine children. The wealthy Trasks buy the most fertile land, but despite its rich soil and plentiful water, the farm remains uncultivated for decades after Cathy abandons Adam.

Good vs. Evil

Steinbeck illustrates the central theme of good versus evil through two of his primary characters: Samuel Hamilton, who represents goodness, and Cathy Ames, who represents pure evil. Both characters play crucial roles in the spiritual development of the protagonist, Adam Trask.

Samuel Hamilton, the positive patriarch, mentors Adam with support and guidance, unlike Adam's own father, Cyrus, who lies about his military record to amass a fortune. Samuel, an Irish immigrant himself, views books as treasures, and fathers nine children. Throughout the novel, he is associated with light, water, and fertitility.

Cathy Ames is Samuel Hamilton's polar opposite. She murders her parents, becomes a prostitute and brothel owner, enslaves her whores with drugs, encourages sadomasochistic sexual practices, and blackmails her customers. In contrast to Samuel, Cathy is associated with darkness and gloom.

Both the innate goodness of Samuel Hamilton and the inherent evil of Cathy Ames deeply influence Adam Trask, and throughout the novel he wavers between the two poles. He loves his wife Cathy even when he is confronted with her evil nature, but also deeply admires his teacher and mentor, Samuel.

Timshel

The concept of *timshel* is a major thematic concern throughout the novel. A hebrew verb, timshel translates into "thou mayest", and expresses the notion that humans have the ability to choose good over evil. It holds that we can decide not to be influenced by our dark family histories, and choose instead to live more positive lives.

The concept of timshel stipulates that every individual, at any given time, has the ability to choose good over evil. This idea is particularly pertinent at the end of the novel, during Adam's death scene. Adam's son Cal believes that he is condemned to become an evil man because he has inhertited his prostitute mother's innately evil nature. Adam, however, raises his hand in blessing and utters the word to his son – timshel – signifying the fact Cal can decide his own moral destiny for himself.

Sibling Rivalry

Steinbeck employs the theme of rivalry to the relationships between the novel's two sets of brothers: Charles and Adam, and Cal and Aron, whose initials recall the biblical brothers Cain and Abel. The sons of Adam and Eve, Cain is a farmer and Abel a shepherd. God prefers Abel's sacrificial offering of a lamb over Cain's offering of grain. In a jealous rage, Cain murders his brother. Cain angrily replies to God's inquiry by saying, "Am I my brother's keeper?" Cain is exiled to wander in the East of Eden.

Charles and Adam's lives and actions recall those of Cain and Abel. When Cyrus favors Adam's birthday gift over Charles', the jealous Charles nearly kills Adam. The next generation of brothers, Cal and Aron, further perpetuates the Cain and Abel legend. When their father, Adam, spurns Cal's birthday present of $15,000, the jealous Cal takes revenge on Aron by taking him to see their mother, a prostitute. Aron joins the army, and soon after dies.

Fatherhood

Steinbeck creates two important father figures in the novel: Samuel Hamilton and Cyrus Trask. Both of these father–figures influence the protagonist, Adam Trask, and present him with paternal models for the choices he must make in his own life. Both Samuel and Cyrus are bearded, in the biblical patriarchal style.

Adam's father, Cyrus, commits the novel's original sin by lying about his Civil War record to advance himself politically and financially. Samuel, on the other hand, is the archetypical force for goodness – the good father to Cyrus' bad father. He exhibits enormous physical strength and capability, while Cyrus hobbles on one leg. Samuel is a symbol of life, of fertility: he cultivates barren soil, fathers nine children, and is associated with water imagery. He digs wells, is always washing, and delivers the twins, Aron and Cal.

Cyrus, on the other hand, is a negative force: a cruel, one–legged thief, Cyrus continually manipulates those around him. He is associated with disease and death, rather than fertility. He infects his religious wife with syphilis, causing her to commit suicide.

Truth

Throughout *East of Eden*, characters withold the truth both from themselves and from others. Cyrus lies about his Civil War record to win an important job and an ill–gained fortune. Charles withholds the truth about Cathy's seduction on Adam's wedding night. Lee lies to himself about his desire to leave the Trask family and open a bookstore. Cal keeps his business ventures secret from his father. Adam and Lee keep the truth about their mother, Cathy, from Cal and Aron. Similarly, Cal fails to inform his father and Lee that he knows that his mother is a notorious brothel owner. Adam lies to himself about Cathy and excuses her depraved behavior.

However, the truth ultimately sets Adam and Cal free. Cathy, the ultimate liar, is suspicious of Adam when he arrives to inform her that Charles has left her a large inheritance. She is used to dealing with people who lie. When he finally faces the truth about her, he feels exhilarated and free. When Cal faces up to the fact that telling Aron the truth might have resulted in his death, he takes responsibility for his actions, and realizes that he has the ability to make good choices in the future.

The Sins of the Father

Throughout the novel, Steinbeck questions the biblical statement that the sins of the father are visited upon the son (Psalms 79:8). Early on, Cyrus Trask lies about his military record in the American Civil War to gain an important government position in Washington D.C. When he dies, he leaves his children, Charles and Adam, an ill–gained fortune. It might seem that Charles and Adam are doomed to live difficult lives because of their father's original sin. Indeed, Charles lives a miserly existence as a laboring recluse on the New England family farm and never knows a moment of happiness, while Adam, too miserable to return home, wanders as a vagabond and marries the ultimate evil female, Cathy Ames.

Cyrus's sin does indeed seem to have filtered down to the next generation. The deeply devout Aron attempts to escape his legacy, but death comes early, on a battlefield in France during World War I. Cal, it seems, is similarly doomed to immorality by his mother's depraved spirit – he earns $15,000 by taking advantage of farmers during the war. He blames himself for his brother's death until Lee helps him understand that God gave people the ability to choose goodness over evil. Cal can undo the family curse and live a morally upright life.

Glossary of Terms

abysmal

very bad; without hope; terrible

barbarism

savagery

deter

restrain; resist

elixir

delicious drink; healthful drink

four bits

fifty cents

hard–pan

rock layer

hell–bent

determined; stubborn; unstoppable

indecipherable

impossible to read; puzzling

intermeshed

intermingled; mixed

jailbird

prisoner

mare

female horse

marksman

expert shooter

mend

fix; repair; sew

outskirts

immediately outside

paradox

contradiction; irony

pummeled

beaten

quarter–section

small area of land

regiment

troop of soldiers

salinas

salt

san Quentin

prison

sanctuary

safe place

six bits

seventy–five cents

syphilis

venereal disease

taciturn

quiet; instrospective

tallow

fat used for candles

thunderhead

dark cloud

timshel

Hebrew verb meaning “thou mayest”

translucent

semi–transparent; limited ability to see

two bits

a quarter

unkempt

untidy; dirty; disheveled

weathered

survived; aged

weltschmertz

painful world; depression; melancholia

Short Summary

Spanning the period between the American Civil War and World War I, *East of Eden* presents two generations of brothers as they battle between good and evil. The first generation consists of the placid Adam Trask and his hot–tempered brother Charles, and the second generation is made up of Adam's sons, the fair–haired, mild–mannered Aron and the dark–haired, quick–tempered Cal. Deeply influenced by the biblical story of Cain and Abel, the novel begins in California's Salinas Valley, where the young narrator was born. He recounts the story of his Irish grandparents, Samuel and Liza Hamilton, who settle in the Salinas Valley, where they meet the members of the Trask family.

The first part of the novel concerns the first generation of Trask brothers, Adam and Charles, and Adam's wife, Cathy Ames (who is referred to as "Kate" in the second part of the book). Cyrus Trask, the one–legged, crooked father, commits the "original sin" that inspires the action of the novel. Cyrus loves his son Adam more than his other son, Charles, and favors Adam's gift of a puppy over Charles's gift of an expensive knife. Tormented by jealousy, Charles savagely beats his brother. Cyrus also lies about his Civil War record to win an important job in Washington D.C. Through his crooked financial dealings, he is able to leave his sons an inheritance of $100,000, which Adam finds out about when he returns from the army. Meanwhile, the most evil character in the novel, Cathy Ames, murders her parents by setting fire to their home. She then becomes the mistress of Mr. Edwards, who runs a ring of prostitutes. Adam marries Cathy soon after she wanders unto his farm, near–dead from a beating suffered at the hands of Edwards. Together, they move to Salinas, where they employ the Chinese–American Lee as a cook and housekeeper, and get to know the much–beloved Samuel Hamilton, who mentors and guides Adam. In Salinas, Cathy gives birth to twin sons, Aron and Cal, and almost immediately abandons her family to return to prostitution, but only after shooting Adam when he attempts to stop her. Soon afterwards, she poisons Faye, the brothel–owner, in an attempt to take over the business. She gives her whores drugs, encourages sadomasochistic sexual practices, and blackmails her customers.

The next part of the novel centers on Adam's children, Aron and Cal, and on Abra Bacon, who falls in love with both brothers. At heart a scholar, Lee raises the twins and remains a constant friend to his employer, Adam Trask, and to their neighbor, Samuel Hamilton, who is raising nine children himself. After a scholarly discussion with Adam and Samuel, Lee researches the Cain and Abel biblical story and proffers the novel's central concept of timshel ("thou mayest"). As the twins grow older, Aron and Cal vie for their father's affection, much as Adam and Charles did earlier. Cal is by far the more complex brother, and knows full well that his father loves Aron more because he resembles their mother. As a teenager, Cal gambles, visits brothels, and is consumed by jealousy over Abra Bacon's love for Aron. Meanwhile, Aron falls in love with Abra, who returns his childish love but realizes later on that Aron, who plans to enter the ministry, is only in love with her glorified image. The daughter of a crooked Salinas politician, Abra comes to love Cal instead, and like him, wonders whether a parent's evil nature can be inherited. In an attempt to gain his father's love, Cal decides to go into business to raise $15,000 to recover his father Adam's business losses. The monetary gift, however, results in disaster: Adam reacts violently when he learns that Cal took advantage of farmers during war–time in an effort to make the money. However, like his father before him, Adam fails to see the love behind his son's gift. In a jealous rage, Cal decides to take Aron to their mother's brothel. All the while, Aron had believed his mother to be dead, and when he finds out otherwise, he runs away, joins the Army during World War I, and dies soon after. After meeting Aron, Cathy commits suicide.

Ultimately, *East of Eden* deals with themes of intergenerational sin, consequent guilt, redemption and forgiveness. Adam suffers a stroke after hearing of Aron's death, and Cal feels overwhelmed with guilt. The negative family legacy is stopped dead in its tracks, however, when Cal is offered surcease from his guilt. His father Adam lifts his hand in a final blessing and utters the word "timshel", the Hebrew word for "thou mayest". Finally, Cal realizes that he is not predestined to live a life of evil, but has the free will to choose goodness and morality.

Summary and Analysis of Chapters 1–8

While growing up in California's Salinas Valley, the narrator learns to tell East from the bright Gabilan Mountains, and West from the dark Santa Lucias Mountains. Although the weather is cyclic – years of heavy rainfall followed by drought – the changes nevertheless surprise the Valley's inhabitants. The area was settled first by Native Americans, who were followed by the Spanish, and finally by the Americans. The narrator's grandparents, Samuel Hamilton and Liza Hamilton (named for Steinbeck's own grandparents), emigrate from Ireland in 1870 and are forced for financial reasons to settle on the Valley's most barren land, where they work hard to raise their nine children. Samuel's good nature and work ethic and Liza's good–heart endear them to their neighbors, especially the Trasks.

After moving from New England, Adam Trask settles in a far more fertile section of the Salinas Valley. As a child, he lived with Cyrus, his Civil War veteran father, his timid stepmother, Alice, and his cruel half–brother, Charles. His deeply devout mother committed suicide upon learning that Cyrus had infected her with syphilis. Cyrus also lied about his military record and moved to Washington D.C. to take a high–ranking government position. The boys had an extremely difficult childhood, but while Adam remains passive, Charles is aggressive, and beats his bother severely after Adam defeats him in a simple game. One day, Adam discovers his stepmother standing by herself and smiling, and begins to leave her presents that she believes come from Charles. His father attempts to convince Adam to join the Army, but thinks that his other son's nature is too inherently dark for such a career. Charles becomes deeply resentful when Cyrus ignores the knife he has given him for his birthday, preferring the puppy given to him by Adam. In a jealous rage, Charles attacks Adam and leaves him unconscious on the road. While Adam recuperates, Cyrus enlists him in the Army.

A self–educated immigrant from Ireland, Samuel Hamilton initially inspires suspicion amongst his new neighbors. However, in time he wins them all over with his warmth, wit, and practical know–how. Samuel and Liza Hamilton never acquire wealth, but they are rich in other ways: they have nine loving children, and a wonderful home life. Liza, the level–headed mother, works from sun–up to sun–down. She pretends to be tough in an effort to control her impractical inventor husband and her large brood of children, but she has a kind heart.

While the Hamiltons are working hard settling in the Salinas Valley, the Trask brothers remain in the East. After the savage beating from Charles, Adam joins the army, while his brother remains on the family farm. Their father, Cyrus, moves to Washington D.C. to take a high–level job in the Office of the Secretary of War. While his brother Adam is absent, Charles suffers a farm accident which leaves him with a dark brown scar on his face. Embarrassed by his scar and reticent by nature, Charles becomes even more reclusive, and longs for Adam's return. However, Adam finds the idea of returning to the farm unpalatable and re–enlists in the Army. At this point, his father sends for him, and Adam finds Cyrus living luxuriously in Washington D.C. with a new prosthetic leg. His father attempts to convince Adam to enroll at West Point Academy, but Adam refuses. Once more, Adam finds that he cannot return home after his second stint in the Army expires, and so he wanders around the country as a vagabond until he is arrested and placed on a chain gang. He writes to Charles to inform him that he has escaped, and asks him to send money so that he can return home. Upon his arrival, he learns that Cyrus has died and left the brothers a fortune of $100,000. Charles tells Adam that their father lied about his war record, and suggests that their inheritance is ill–gotten. Adam suggests that they move to California.

In chapter eight, Cathy Ames takes center stage. She has the face of an angel, but the temperament of the devil. Her parents, solid middle–class folk, adore their only child and cannot come to terms with her evil nature. The girl has an uncanny, almost preternatural ability to sexually attract men. Indeed, when she is only twelve she seduces a group of teenage boys and arranges for her mother to discover them just to see the boys suffer the consequences. Later, one of Cathy's teachers commits suicide after a mysterious liaison with her. Cathy has an intense hatred for her parents that seems wholly unfounded, but rather than just running away, she chooses to burn down their house, and they die in the flames. The neighbors are left thinking Cathy has also perished in the fire.

Analysis

John Steinbeck, who casts himself as the young narrator, carefully creates the near–mythical setting in which the characters of *East of Eden* reside. His setting, however, does far more than merely serve as the backdrop for the action. Indeed, the setting creates thematic tension and opposition. Steinbeck sets up the biblical metaphor of good versus evil (or light versus dark) – the novel's central theme – by utilizing Salinas Valley, California, where he lived as a youngster, as the novel's primary setting. "Evil", or darkness, is represented by the Santa Lucias Mountains, which lie to the West, while "good", or light, is represented by the Gabilan Mountains, to the East. It is here, between these two mountain ranges, that the Hamilton and Trask families settle. Although the eleven–member Hamilton family is certainly fertile, they are forced to live on the most barren land in the Valley, while the dysfunctional, almost infertile Trask family lives on the Valley's richest land. This discrepancy is a physical manifestation of the fact that the strong immigrants, Samuel and Liza Hamilton, are forced to eke out a living on next to nothing, while the rich but weak Trasks, who inherited their wealth through dishonest means, seem to be sliding into degeneracy. Both the Hamiltons and the Trasks are led by heavily bearded men (Samuel and Cyrus, respectively), but the men are very different types of patriarchs: Samuel is the loving, healthy, "good" father, while Cyrus is the hateful, diseased, "bad" father. The kindly Samuel provides Adam with a positive paternal role model, but the "sins" of Adam's biological father nevertheless wreak havoc upon him and his brother, Charles.

Adam and Charles are representations of the biblical Cain and Abel, as evidenced both by their initials and their family circumstances. In the Bible, Abel's sacrifice of a lamb pleases God more than Cain's gift of grain, and Cain murders his brother in a jealous rage. God curses Cain and sends him out into the land of Nod, which lies to the East of Eden (the location referred to in the title of Steinbeck's novel). Like Cain, Charles becomes deeply jealous when their father, Cyrus, ignores Charles' expensive gift in favor of the free mongrel puppy given to him by his favored son, Adam. In a rage, Charles attacks Adam and leaves him unconscious.

The biblical tale of Cain and Abel informs the plot of the entire novel. Elements of the story are found in two generations of Trasks: Charles and Adam, and Adam's twin sons, Cal and Aron. In addition, the story goes on to be discussed for years by Adam, Lee, and Samuel Hamilton, as the three men attempt to come to terms with life's ongoing battle between good and evil. The scar resulting from Charles' farm accident is emblematic of an element in the Cain and Abel story. As part of God's punishment for Abel's murder, God places a similar scar on Cain as a warning for others to avoid him, and curses him to wander the earth for the rest of his days. In *East of Eden*, Charles is the one with the scar, while it is his brother Adam who wanders the earth, first as an officer in the army, and later as a vagabond. Adam eventually returns home, marries Cathy Ames, and moves to California.

In addition to the Cain and Abel paradigm, *East of Eden* (along with many of John Steinbeck's other novels) is replete with biblical allusions. Of particular note is the concept of original sin, as found in Genesis. Just as Adam and Eve committed the original sin by disobeying God and eating the forbidden apple in the Garden of Eden, Cyrus, the father of Charles and Adam, commits the novel's original sin by lying about his war record and acquiring money through false pretenses. Likewise, just as the descendants of Adam and Eve were cursed for the sins of their forebears, so too are the sins of the father visited upon Cyrus' descendents. Despite their large inheritance, Charles and Adam are reclusive and miserable.

Cathy Ames, whose "aims" are evil, is a representative of the Biblical antihero, Satan. Manipulative and uncaring, she seduces people into obeying her wishes. This character has been criticized by scholars for not seeming "real" enough; indeed, she fails to demonstrate even a single positive characteristic to counteract her evil traits, and at no point in this long novel does the reader ever feel one iota of sympathy towards her. Steinbeck never offers an explanation for why she burns her parents to death, seduces teenage boys, or compels her teacher to commit suicide. For Cathy, evil simply comes naturally. Later in the novel, Samuel Hamilton comes to realize that Cathy lacks some essential human element.

Summary and Analysis of 9–15

Cathy Ames reemerges as Catherine Amesbury after setting fire to her parents' house and leaving them for dead. She approaches Mr. Edwards, who runs a prostitute ring in New England, seeking a job. His devout wife believes that he runs a respectable business; at home, Mr. Edwards is the epitome of the middle–class family man. Mr. Edwards is shocked by Cathy's request, because she is far more beautiful and upscale than the other women who work for him. He treats his employees poorly, and controls them with an iron fist. However, for the first time in his life he falls in love: he becomes obsessed with Cathy and takes her as his mistress, buying her a luxurious house. However, when he comes to realize the extent of his dependency upon her, he has her investigated and learns about the suspicious nature of the fire that killed her parents. At this point, he comes to see her true nature. One evening, he takes her out into the country, beats her almost to the point of death, and leaves her near the Trask farm.

Although they never need to work, Charles and Adam maintain the Connecticut family farm, constantly bickering amongst themselves over silly, inconsequential things such as what time to set the alarm clock, or what to cook for dinner. One day, Adam leaves in a huff, travels to South America, and returns to find an even larger farm. Charles now works on from sun–up to sun–down. Soon afterwards, they find Cathy unconscious on their back steps. Despite Charles' protests that it would be unseemly for two single men to house a single, unrelated woman, Adam nurses her back to health. Soon, he finds that he has fallen deeply in love with her, and asks her to marry him. When the sheriff hears about her broken bones and bruises, he calls to question her, but she feigns amnesia. Charles is one of the few characters who can clearly see through Cathy's wiles, and she fears him for it. He becomes furious when Adam announces their engagement. On their wedding night, Cathy drugs Adam with the opiate medication she has been taking for pain, and seduces Charles. Charles, who puts up no resistance, calls Adam a "poor bastard" as he takes his brother's wife into his bed. A short time later, Adam and Charles move to California.

In the transitional chapter before Adam and Cathy Trask take up residence in the Salinas Valley, the narrator looks back from the beginning of the twentieth century, pondering humanity's ability to view history through rose–colored lenses and failure to recall disagreeable historical facts. He summarizes the previous century as: "boom and bust, bankruptcy, depression." People either idealize the past ("the old time, the gay time, sweet and simple, as though time were young and fearless") or they say "good riddance," and look eagerly forward to "this clean new hundred years." It is this tendency to forget, he continues, that enables the progression of the human race. He goes on to declare that the nineteenth century was an era of chaos, and predicts that the advance of automation during the twentieth century will result in a loss of creativity on the individual level. "Monstrous changes," he states, "are taking place in the world, and mass culture will deeply affect the individual mind, which will be caught up in the collective mentality: when our food and clothing and housing are all born in the complication of mass production, mass method is bound to get into our thinking and to eliminate all other thinking." Only individuals, he holds, can create; groups of people have never created anything. The most valuable thing in the world, the narrator believes, is the individual mind.

Before they leave for California, Adam buys out Charles' share of the family farm and moves with the reluctant Cathy to the Salinas Valley, in California. Adam remains blind to the evil that permeates Cathy's being: he views her as "a sweet and holy girl, precious beyond thinking, clean and loving." To her dismay, Cathy discovers that she is pregnant – a condition she finds absolutely abhorrent – and attempts to abort the baby herself by using a knitting needle. She fails in her attempt, and lies to the doctor, saying that she is terrified of passing along epilepsy to any offspring. The doctor informs Adam of Cathy's pregnancy, and he practically leaps with joy. Finally, he is happy, and feels that life is worth living. Full of hope, he goes about setting up a ranch so that he can gain from the rich opportunities all around him. Samuel Hamilton comes to help Adam locate a ranch with water. Like his biblical namesake, Adam is intent on building a garden in his new–found Eden: "I mean to make a garden of my land." Samuel is a diviner with an almost preternatural ability to locate water. While they explore the Salinas Valley for the most fertile piece of land available, Samuel and Adam form an instant friendship that will last a lifetime. At Samuel's prompting, Adam buys the old Sanchez place, located near King City.

In chapter 14, Steinbeck departs from the intertwining Hamilton and Trask family narratives to honor the schoolteacher Olive Hamilton: one of Samuel Hamilton's daughters, and Steinbeck's real–life mother. The wife of a flour mill owner, Olive sells the most Liberty bonds during World War I, and earns the grand prize of a ride in an airplane. The young mother is terrified, and absolutely convinced that she is going to die. She prepares for her death by completing any unfinished business, burning letters, and donning new underwear. Olive willingly undergoes all of this mental torture simply to make her family proud. She sits in the seat behind the pilot, and they take off, to her children's absolute delight. When the pilot suggests some daredevil maneuvers, Olive cannot hear him over the noise, and just waves and smiles in acquiescence. No matter what type of stunts the pilot practices, she merely smiles. Underneath the smiling veneer, however, she is in shock, and is nearly catatonic when she comes back down to earth. Her trip turns into a much–repeated family story.

Steinbeck takes back up the threads of Adam and Cathy Trask's story in chapter 15. Sadly deluded by his wife Cathy, Adam continues to find happiness on his new California ranch, and eagerly looks forward to the birth of his first child. He has almost forgotten the dark days he spent on the Connecticut family farm, and no longer corresponds by mail with his brother Charles. His Chinese–American servant, Lee, becomes indispensable to him. Cathy doesn't like Lee, but realizes how invaluable a good servant can be and puts up with him. Like Samuel Hamilton and Charles Trask before him, Lee can see through Cathy, and since she cannot control him, she fears him. Lee speaks in a degrading stereotypical Chinese pidgin dialect and wears his hair long despite his university education simply because Americans expect him to do so. Americans look at him suspiciously if he speaks as they do. The dialect helps to keep him from being singled out; in a sense, it makes him invisible. Lee also becomes fast friends with Samuel Hamilton who, since both men are immigrants, treats him as an equal. Lee explains to Samuel the pride he takes in his choice of occupation: "A good servant, and I am an excellent one, can completely control his master." Samuel accepts Adam's proffered invitation to dinner at the ranch, but leaves in a hurry when Cathy doesn't speak. Something, he realizes, is very wrong, yet Adam sits at the table as if all is normal, completely enthralled with his beautiful wife. After Samuel leaves, Cathy announces to Adam that she plans on leaving him as soon as possible after giving birth. Adam, believing that pregnant women have silly ideas and that all will be well once the baby arrives, dismisses her announcement.

Analysis

For Steinbeck, *East of Eden* was an experimental work of fiction which intertwined the strands of two family narratives, with chapters on philosophy and family history. He received both negative criticism and high literary acclaim from scholars for this methodology. So, while the structure may initially seem choppy and the timeline difficult to follow, readers may eventually come to recognize Steinbeck's vision and begin viewing the novel in terms of its organic unity.

While Charles and Adam represent the biblical brothers Cain and Abel, Cathy Amesbury, whose new name suggests that her evil "aims" have been "buried", represents Satan, who tempted Adam and Eve to eat the apple from the tree of knowledge in the Garden of Eden, despite God's injunction against such an action. Cathy tempts Adam Trask sexually until he marries her, and shortly thereafter, she causes his downfall. Cathy and Charles hate each other, each recognizing the evil inherent within the other. In this manner, they are kindred spirits. Cathy's behavior is unsurprising given her past actions against her parents, friends, schoolteacher, and Mr. Edwards, but Charles' betrayal of his brother demonstrates his profoundly evil nature. "I think you are a devil," he states earlier to Cathy. Clearly, when Charles accepts his brother's wife into his bed on Adam's wedding night, he is, in effect, sleeping with the devil.

In the transitional, highly philosophical chapter 12, Steinbeck insists on the primacy of the creative power of the individual mind, and warns of the danger of following the impulse of the destructive crowd. The power of the individual mind is, he maintains, indomitable. Although it will not be apparent for awhile, here Steinbeck lays the foundation for one of the novel's major themes – the issue of free will. Are people, he wonders, born with an innate predisposition towards good or evil, or do they have the ability to choose between the two extremes? Forgoing predestination, he leans toward the primacy of individual choice; hence, he develops his fear that the individual mind will be caught up in the threatening collective mentality.

Steinbeck moves – somewhat awkwardly – from this philosophical section of the novel to a eulogy in praise of his mother. Although the chapter concerning Olive Hamilton seems out–of–place because it is "out of time" in terms of the chronological narrative, Steinbeck has a two–fold reason for placing it in this section of the novel. Besides honoring his mother, the author juxtaposes the good mother, Olive, who would die rather than disappoint her family, with the evil mother, Cathy Trask. Olive comes from the fertile, fun–loving, happy Hamilton family, and becomes the highly efficient, loving mother of the four Steinbeck children. She is very much like her mother, Liza Hamilton. Cathy, on the other hand, murders her parents and attempts to abort her first child. One of the novel's themes, fertility versus barrenness, resonates in the juxtaposition of these two female characters. Thus, the admirable Olive Hamilton acts as a foil for the deviant Cathy Trask in same manner as the servant Lee, who will come in time to serve the twins in a maternal capacity.

The Chinese–American Trask's servant, Lee, is in fact a philosopher in disguise. An extraordinarily deep thinker, he sees through people without being observed, and acts as a foil to the novel's evil characters, especially Cathy. Steinbeck also takes this opportunity to shed light on the plight of Asian–Americans, who have a considerably difficult time assimilating into mainstream American culture.

Summary and Analysis of Chapters 16–22

Although he is at heart a positive, sunny character, Samuel Hamilton sinks into a deep depression as he returns home from dinner at the Trask ranch. As his faithful horse pulls his cart home on a star–studded evening, Samuel begins feeling unwell, and recalls a time during his youth in Ireland when he went with his father to town, where they saw a handsome young man being excoriated by a crowd. Samuel shudders as he recalls the man's inhuman eyes – the same merciless eyes that he has just encountered in the visage of Cathy Trask: "The eyes of Cathy had no message, no communication of any kind. There was nothing recognizable behind them. They were not human eyes." The man Samuel saw as a child was executed in front of him because he was thought to be evil incarnate, a devil in human form. Try as he might, Samuel cannot get the horrible image out of his mind. He remembers how the man was thought to be lacking an essential human component, and realizes that Cathy Trask is similarly without this crucial element. When he returns home he is glad to see his practical wife, Liza, and informs her that – despite her advice to the contrary – he has agreed to help Adam rebuild his ranch. Some time later, Samuel, who delivered his own children, is called upon to help Cathy when she goes into early labor. On their way to the ranch house, Samuel and his Chinese–American friend Lee, who is the Trasks' servant, share their similarly negative feelings about Cathy. At the house, they find Adam fretting, and ask the nervous father–to–be to leave. Samuel finds Cathy in a darkened room and opens the blind to let in light, making her diabolically angry. She hates Samuel, and bites him when he attempts to comfort her during her labor. After giving birth to twin boys, Cathy refuses to see them or nurse them. Samuel is shocked by Cathy's unnatural behavior and sends for Liza to help. Cathy informs Adam of her plans to leave within a week after giving birth. He dismisses her words as ravings brought on by the trauma of childbirth, but later she proves him wrong, shooting him in the arm when he attempts to stop her. Horace Quinn, the local deputy, refuses to believe that the shooting was an accident – especially when he learns that Cathy has left the ranch. He informs the Salinas sheriff, who has heard that Cathy is working in Faye's brothel, about the events. They decide to keep Cathy's whereabouts secret from Adam to protect the children from the knowledge that their mother is a prostitute. Samuel and Adam become close friends while Adam recovers. The older man tells Adam that he too has suffered, and assures him that by going through the motions of living he will heal in time. Adam has no idea that his wife is still in Salinas, residing in a house of prostitution.

The houses of prostitution in the Salinas Valley attract a variety of clientele by specializing in different sexual fantasies. Faye's, the brothel where Cathy (now "Kate") winds up, provides homey comfort in addition to sexual release, but does not condone any extreme sexual practices. Faye is well–liked by the authorities because she keeps an eye out for the criminal element amongst her clients and donates money to the local charities. Kate endears herself to Faye, and quickly becomes indispensable to the older woman. She organizes the house, ingratiates herself to the other girls, improves the menu and working conditions, and saves Faye a great deal of money. The sheriff, whom Kate likes for his direct and truthful manner, pays a visit to Kate after hearing of Adam's shooting, but cannot do much because Adam has not pressed charges. The sheriff warns Kate to keep a low profile, and to stay away from her sons – and his own son, for that matter. In addition, he orders her to dye her hair black so that she will not be recognized.

Eventually, Kate becomes so indispensable to Faye that she begins to think of her as her own daughter. At a private party, she informs Kate that she wants her to stop working as a prostitute: "You could take care of things for me and not go upstairs." She informs Kate that she wishes to be called "mother", and tells her that she is the sole beneficiary in her will, ordering Kate to drink champagne to celebrate. Kate, who loses control when she drinks, becomes hostile, calls Faye a fat worm, and lets slip that she has, unbeknownst to Faye, been making a lot of extra money by engaging in lucrative sadomasochistic sexual adventures with clients who ask for such services. Gone is the good daughter routine, and the vile being that lies underneath the facade is now apparent to all. Faye is horrified by the revelation. However, after Kate sobers up, she drugs Faye with an opiate and convinces her upon waking that the happenings of the night before were all part of a bad dream. The distraught Faye, who wants more than anything to be cared for and loved, believes Kate. At this point, Kate takes control of the brothel and begins to poison Faye. She feigns illness herself so that Doctor Wilde will provide her with the medication she needs to kill Faye, thus making it appear as though her death is the result of natural causes. When Faye dies, Kate buries the bottles of poisonous medication in the backyard. To observers, she appears to be a distraught daughter, abject with grief. She loses weight and takes to her bed, and her devotion goes unquestioned. The entire time in the brothel, Kate never once thinks of Adam Trask or her twin boys.

In the wake of Cathy's departure, Adam sinks deeper and deeper into lethargy and despair. After more than a year has gone by, Lee complains to his friend Samuel Hamilton that Adam has not yet even named his twin sons. Lee has, in effect, become the boys' mother *and* father – they have even begun to say Chinese words. Samuel Hamilton comes immediately, and finds Adam deep in depression, seemingly unable (or, Samuel thinks, unwilling) to help himself: "It seemed to Samuel that Adam might be pleasuring himself with sadness." However, after a few failed attempts at talking to Adam, Samuel hits his friend to jolt him out of his despair. Lee, by now speaking proper English, joins Samuel and Adam for a drink while the babies sleep in the warm dust. The men begin an intellectual discussion about the story of Cain and Abel, and analyze the continuing human cycle of rejection, anger, revenge, and guilt. Although Samuel suggests the names Cain and Abel for the boys, they decide to call the children Caleb (after the man who made it to the Promised Land) and Aaron, who failed in the attempt. Over time, the names morph into Cal and Aron.

Analysis

Steinbeck continues to juxtapose good characters with evil characters in an effort illustrate one of the novel's primary themes: the battle between good and evil. The upright, honest Samuel, who symbolizes God the Father, becomes severely ill after the satanic Cathy bites him on the hand when he attempts to help her during labor. Here, good clashes directly with evil, and the poisonous Cathy's evil is so powerful that it incapacitates – indeed, almost kills – Samuel Hamilton, who is goodness personified. Samuel must turn to his benevolent wife, Liza, to give him strength and restore him. As they are both mother–figures, there is an inevitable contrast between Liza and Cathy: Liza is a self–sacrificing, adoring mother, while Cathy refuses to look upon her children's faces or care for them, and even abandons them as soon as she is physically capable of doing so. Not for a single instant does she consider her children's well–being. Liza, the loving mother of nine, arrives to save the day: she, it seems, is the only one capable of curing Samuel of the damage done to him by the evil Cathy. Along with Lee, she helps care for the newborn twins. Liza's relentless cleaning of Cathy's newly renovated home signifies that the Trask house is dirty and diseased.

Steinbeck has received a great deal of negative criticism for this dramatic juxtaposition of good and evil characters. His characters, many scholars maintain, are simply not real enough to be convincing. However, it could be argued this is exactly what Steinbeck set out to accomplish, because he wanted to reach as many people as possible and have his stories impact them in the manner of biblical parables. In *East of Eden*, he offers a simplistic personification of good versus evil (Samuel and Liza Hamilton versus Cathy Trask). Similarly, Quinn and the sheriff are cast as good characters, almost guardian angels, who protect the Trask babies from contamination by their evil mother. In addition, the sheriff is cast as a good father (in contrast to the weak, incapacitated Adam) when he warns Kate to stay away from the twins and from his own son.

Faye is an interesting character: although she is a brothel owner, there is nothing inherently evil about her. In fact, she gives more money to the local charities than most business owners. She also views her girls in an almost motherly fashion, and treats her customers well. As the novel progresses, it becomes clear that Faye is intended to be juxtaposed with Kate, who eventually takes over the brothel and runs it in a particularly vile manner.

The juxtaposition of good and evil characters continues with Samuel Hamilton and Adam Trask: Samuel is the epitome of the good father figure, while Adam pays virtually no attention to his children. Samuel fathers nine children, all of whom turn out to be good people. He cares deeply for each, and respects their unique talents and failings. Adam, on the other hand, fails to give his children names even more than a year after their birth. This might suggest that Adam on some level enjoyed his treatment at the hands of the sadistic Cathy. After all, Adam's ongoing despondence over his clearly evil wife leads the reader to wonder if, in the end, he is any better a person than Cathy. Adam grew up under the influence of a particularly cruel father, but seems unable to treat his children any better than he was treated himself.

However, Steinbeck does suggest that people are different in different phases of their lives, and that they have the ability to change. This idea is expanded upon later in the novel through the central concept of *timshel*. Since familial relationships play a particularly important role in this novel, it is especially pertinent to note that Steinbeck's idea of forgiveness holds that individuals have the power to alter family dynamics. At this point, the reader should recall the rejection of Adam's brother Charles by their father Cyrus, which echoed God's rejection of Cain in favor of Abel. Charles' subsequent anger toward Adam nearly resulted in Adam's death. As the novel unfolds, will Adam become a better father, or will the cycle established by Cain and Abel be repeated in the Trask family once more, causing Adam to repeat his father's mistakes?

The biblical story of Cain and Abel, which is thematically central to the novel, is brought into sharper focus in this section. Samuel even suggests naming the children after Cain and Abel, but Adam rejects this morbid idea. Samuel, Adam, and Lee discuss the story at great length, even going so far as to read the Bible. They mull over each word, and wonder aloud why God chose Abel's gift of a lamb over Cain's gift of grain, but cannot find an answer. They also examine God's decision to cast out Cain and force him to wander the earth, discussing what, exactly, God promised Cain. Did God give Cain any hope for the future, or was he forever condemned? If no hope was offered, then are the descendants of mankind doomed to repeat the sins of their fathers over and over again, with redemption forever lying out of reach? During the philosophical debate, Adam argues that repeating the negative cycle of anger, revenge, and subsequent guilt is not preordained. After all, he remarks, he never even considered killing his own brother, Charles. However, he becomes much quieter after recalling the time when his brother almost killed him in a jealous rage.

Summary and Analysis of Chapters 23 –30

Ten years have now passed since Adam, Samuel, and Lee named the Trask children. In the interim, Samuel's favorite child and "greatest joy", Una, has married a photographer named Anderson and moved with him to Oregon. Her husband keeps Una in abject poverty, and she eventually dies (perhaps having committed suicide) after living for years in conditions of hard physical labor and near starvation. Una's death casts Samuel into a depression from which even he cannot emerge. He wrongfully blames himself for having neglected his beloved daughter. This is the beginning of his decline: "his young skin turned old, his clear eyes dulled." Samuel's other eight children (including Steinbeck's mother, Olive) meet to discuss what should be done about their aging parents, and decide to have them visit in turns under the guise of wishing to spend more time with them. Tom Hamilton, upset about the idea of his parents leaving the family farm, sees this strategy as insulting to his father, but Samuel assures him that he knows quite well what is going on, and that he has neither the energy nor the inclination to fight it: "I know why I'm going — and, Tom, I know where I'm going, and I am content." The "why" and the "where" here indicate that Samuel knows full well that he will die shortly. He visits his old neighbors, who are strewn about the Salinas Valley, and saves the Trask ranch for last. On what will be his final visit, he finds that the twins he once delivered are now eleven years old. Once again, the story of Cain and Abel comes up over drinks. Lee explains that in the ten year hiatus, he has studied the Cain and Abel story in Genesis 4: 1–16 with four Chinese sages and a rabbi in San Francisco. In one biblical translation, Lee explains, God promises Cain that in time he will overcome sin, but in another translation, God *orders* Cain to overcome sin. After ten years of intellectual sparring, the scholars conclude that both translations are in error and that, indeed, the Hebrew word *timshel*, the verb in question, actually means "thou mayest" – in other words, thou mayest rule over sin. As Samuel declares, it is "the choice of winning." Samuel immediately grasps the meaning of the term, to Lee's great delight: God simply gave human beings the ability to choose good over evil. By choosing good, they can rule over evil. At this point, Samuel makes a decision about a secret that has been plaguing him for years. Now able to look death directly in the face, Samuel decides to save Adam from his ongoing apathy and dejection by informing him that his wife still resides in Salinas, where she runs a notorious whorehouse. Adam, unable to accept what Samuel tells him, runs away into the night, screaming in horror.

Adam attends Samuel's funeral, which is held soon after his death on March 15th, the infamous ides of March. Afterwards, he drinks at the Abbot House bar before going to Kate's brothel to finally confront his wife. For the first time, he sees Cathy/Kate not as a beautiful young woman, but as a vile monster. At last, he feels free, and his dark, depressive mood lifts. Although Kate tempts him sexually, she holds no more power over him. To demonstrate her power over others, she shows him photographs of some of the most important men in town in compromising sexual situations. She plans on blackmailing these men in an effort to raise cash so she can move to New York City. All men, Cathy cries out to Adam, are nasty, selfish brutes. She expects Adam to be impressed with her cleverness, but he is absolutely horrified. He tells her, "you hate something in them you can't understand. You don't hate their evil. You hate the good in them you can't get at." At this point, she screams at him like an animal, declaring that he will one day plead with her to take him back. He tries to leave, and she becomes even more hysterical, screaming at him that she slept with his brother, Charles, and that Adam may not even be the children's father. In response, Adam says that the boys' true parentage simply doesn't matter to him. Before returning home, he decides to buy a car from Samuel's son, Will Hamilton, who is quickly becoming the most important businessman in town. When Adam returns home, he informs Lee about Kate's state of mind: "In some strange way my eyes of cleared." Lee, who sees with great relief that Adam has finally thrown off his cloud of depression, informs Adam that the time has come for him to fulfill his dream of opening a bookstore in San Francisco. Adam agrees, but asks him to remain until he can get his affairs in order. Lee feels confident now that he can begin accomplishing his own dreams instead of spending all his time caring for the Trask twins.

The dark–haired child, Caleb Trask ("Cal"), always wants to fight, while his blonde–haired brother, Aron, only fights when provoked. One day while out hunting rabbits with bows and arrows, they twins argue over who should take credit for having shot a rabbit. Aron is childlike, light–hearted, and naive, while Cal is dark, clever, and manipulative. Cal confides in Aron a secret he overheard from some men in King City: their mother isn't dead after all, but is in fact living in Salinas. Aron, who believes that his mother is in heaven, becomes extremely upset, and vehemently denies his brother's allegation. Cal joyfully realizes that he has found the sharpest weapon of all for controlling his brother: Aron's love for their missing mother. The boys return home to find unexpected company: the Bacons and their beautiful eleven year–old daughter, Abra, have asked for shelter from a sudden rain storm. As the children play outside, Mr. and Mrs. Bacon suggest that Adam move the family to Salinas so the boys can attend school. The boys are completely tongue–tied by the beautiful Abra. Adam goes to his room to get the dead rabbit they killed, placing it tenderly in a box to give to the girl as a gift. He includes a note asking Abra to marry him. Meanwhile, the manipulative Cal scares Abra into thinking there is a snake in the box: she tosses it away, and unknowingly breaks young Aron's heart.

Adam, whose depression has finally lifted, surprises the boys during dinner that night by talking to them. Cal takes this opportunity to inquire about his mother, saying that Abra wants to know where her grave is so that they can take her some flowers. Once again, Adam lies to the boys. Lee, who believes in honesty at all costs, strongly suggests that Adam tell the boys about their mother before they find out about her from strangers and come to hate their father for having kept the truth from them. Lee then shares his personal history: to repay a family debt, Lee's father was forced to leave China and move to America to become an indentured worker building railroads. Unbeknownst to her husband, Lee's mother disguised herself as a man so that she could accompany him to the United States. When they learned that she was pregnant, they planned on going into the mountains, but Lee's father broke his leg, and Lee's mother went into early labor. When the mob of workers found out that there was a woman amongst them, "they all went mad." The men gang–raped and killed Lee's mother shortly after she gave birth to Lee. With great humility, Lee goes on to say that Adam should not judge the men: "No child ever had such care as I." After Lee's story, Adam becomes melancholy and writes to Charles, inviting him to come to California for a visit. He tells him that he and Cathy have separated, that she lives in town, and that he sees her on occasion. A week following the arrival of his new car, Adam drives to the post office, where he finds a letter announcing the death of his brother. Just like their father Cyrus, Charles has left an inheritance of $100,000 to be divided between Adam and Cathy. Later that evening, Cal eavesdrops on a conversation between Adam and Lee, and learns that his mother is not only alive, but that she lives in Salinas and works in a whorehouse. Cal, horrified, drops to his knees and begs God for forgiveness and to make him a better person.

Analysis 23–30

Steinbeck, who positions the biblical story of Cain and Abel at the center of *East of Eden*, explores the concept of *timshel* – the key to true redemption for the characters in the novel. After a ten–year hiatus, Samuel, Adam, and Lee return to the philosophical conversation they previously debated at length. Lee tells the other two gentlemen that for the last ten years he has been studying the Cain and Abel story in Genesis 4: 1–16 with a group of scholars in San Francisco. In one biblical translation, Lee points out, Cain is promised by God that he will in time overcome sin. This interpretation casts Cain into a passive light: he is wholly without free will. A different translation states that God *orders* Cain to overcome sin, implying a similar lack of individual agency. These two translations both preclude the possibility of redemption. Lee goes on to explain that both translations are in error, and that the Hebrew verb *timshel* ("thou mayest") suggests a different interpretation of the events. God, Lee believes, told Cain that he could make the *choice* to overcome sin. Mankind has free will, and is not predestined to repeat the sins of the fathers. Samuel is quick to appreciate this concept, and utilizes it as a means to save his friend, Adam Trask. Adam, he feels, must know the truth if he is to be free to choose a different sort of life.

Adam is given the choice to live his life clearly, or to remain bogged down in apathy, depression, and longing for Cathy. Thanks to Lee and Samuel, Adam gains agency through his realization of the novel's central concept, *timshel*, and by learning that his wife is still living in Salinas. Finally, he can choose to live differently, and to see Kate as the monster she is and not as his pretty, young, vulnerable wife. He finds within himself the power to resist her feminine wiles. Indeed, when they at last meet face–to–face he finds that he has all the power, and that for once she is powerless. At this point, Adam finally becomes a real father, a father in the vein of Samuel Hamilton. Now that he has become a good father, it doesn't even matter to Adam that the twins might not be his. His decision to purchase a car and learn to drive it signifies his willingness to move ahead: it is the beginning of a new era for the Trasks. Lee also realizes that he is finally free to move. The deep freeze imparted by the evil ice witch Kate has melted at last.

In addition to the concept of *timshel*, the novel's central thematic concern – the battle between goodness and evil – rages on in the new generation, and the issue of tainted money once more comes to light. Aron is innocent and good–hearted, and turns away from anything even suggestive of evil. When faced with the truth about his mother, he rejects it entirely, and doesn't even want to discuss the possibility that his mother might still be alive. To consider this possibility would mean that his father might have lied, and this is something he cannot fathom. He is also tenderhearted: he instantly falls in love with Abra, immediately idealizing her and pursuing her hand in marriage. Simply put, Aron is pure at heart. Cal, on the other hand, is darker not just in physiognomy, but also in temperament. He is manipulative, disobedient, seeks out trouble, and has an insatiable curiosity. While Aron accepts what is told to him about his mother at face value, Cal questions everything, and seeks to discover the truth for himself. The reader is left wondering whether the Cain and Abel paradigm will repeat itself. Lee's family saga is a testament to familial love and sacrifice, an illustration of how family members can and should treat one another. Will Cal attempt to kill Aron, as Charles once attempted to kill Adam? Cal's childish jealousy of Aron stems from the fact that Abra favors Aron over him, but hope is found in the fact that Cal is horrified by his actions, and prays for the strength to change.

Money continually interferes with Cal's ability to choose goodness over evil. From early on in life, Cal is attracted to money. Indeed, the first thing that springs to mind when he hears of his uncle's death is money, while Aron thinks about putting flowers on the grave. The ill–gained inheritance Cyrus left to Adam and Charles comes into play once again in this section: their grandfather's "original sin" is revisited upon Cyrus's descendants. Charles leaves Adam and Cathy $100,000, having doubled his inheritance through miserly means. It is worth noting that despite the fact that both inheritances have been earned through corrupt means, neither Adam nor Charles even momentarily considers returning the money. The issue of tainted money circulates throughout the entire novel.

Summary and Analysis of Chapters 31–37

Kate is immediately suspicious when Adam visits her at the whorehouse to inform her of his brother's death and offer her half of the inheritance, $50,000. She exclaims: "I don't know what the trick is, but I'm going to find out." She is simply not used to honest people, and does not know how to act appropriately when she encounters one. Adam informs her that she lacks the ability to perceive goodness and beauty, and that she can only view the dark side of everything. He goes on to tell her that she cannot possibly understand that even the men whose sexually–explicit photographs she secretly possesses also have good facets to their personalities. Mirroring Samuel Hamilton's belief regarding Cathy, Adam remarks, "I think you are only part of a human." Adam senses fear in her, and when she realizes that she can no longer control him, she becomes frustrated and abusive. After he leaves Cathy, Adam visits Samuel's wife, Liza Hamilton, in Salinas. Olive Hamilton opens the door and invites him in, and he meets Olive's children: the young John Steinbeck, and his sister Mary. Liza, who has declined in stature but not in spirit, is glad to see him. He tells her that he is thinking of moving to Salinas so the children can receive a better education, and she suggests that he buy her daughter Dessie's house. Dessie Hamilton, it seems, has decided to close her dress–making business and move back to the family ranch, which her brother Tom Hamilton has run since the death of his father, Samuel.

Tom Hamilton cannot pull himself out of the numbing depression he fell into after his father Samuel's death, but is happy to hear that Dessie plans on returning to the ranch. Dessie was always "the beloved of the family" due to her kindness and unwavering sense of humor. Although she was popular with her customers, her dress–making business suffered with the advance of automation. Tom welcomes her home grandly, with painted signs and the words "Welcome Home" spelled out in white–washed stones. Both of the siblings are happy to be in each other's company, but Dessie suffers from a severe stomach pain that she keeps hidden from Tom. At first, the brother and sister are very happy taking care of the ranch and of each other, but in the evenings they both lie in their beds, severely troubled. Pain continues to invade Dessie's body, and Tom sinks further into depression. They decide to travel, and opt to raise pigs in an effort to finance a trip to Europe. Tom goes to see his businessman brother, Will Hamilton, about a loan. Will is not enthusiastic about the pig proposition, and Tom becomes even more forlorn. He returns home to find Dessie in great physical distress, and gives her a does of salts as medication; later, the doctor tells him that this was the worst thing he could have done. In effect, Tom accidentally causes his beloved sister's death. Afterwards, he sinks even deeper into depression. He begins to go mad and starts talking to his dead father, Samuel, pleading with him to understand that he cannot continue to cope with the vicissitudes of life. "I cannot live," he states to the ghostly Samuel. "I've killed Dessie and I want to sleep." He makes suicide arrangements by writing a letter to his brother, Will, asking him to cover up his death as a riding accident to spare their mother pain, and shoots himself with a Smith and Wesson .38.

In chapter 34, which is the cornerstone of the entire novel and takes place in the wake of the deaths of Charles Trask and four of the Hamiltons (Samuel, Charles, Dessie and Tom), Steinbeck once again interrupts the novel's chronological narrative to bring to light the philosophical insights that resonate throughout. In this chapter, the narrator crystallizes the novel's primary theme: "humans are caught in a net of good and evil." He asserts that there is no other real story in the entire world, and that there never will be. He goes on to declare that it is how we live our simple lives while caught in that trap of good and evil that determines our success as individuals and our impact on the world, and especially on those we leave behind. As examples, he discusses the lives and careers of three men, only one of whom succeeded in traversing life's ups and downs. A person's life, he maintains, can be measured by the feelings of those left behind.

Steinbeck again takes up the chronological thread in Chapter 35. Adam buys Dessie Hamilton's house in Salinas, and Lee, after completing all the work involved in the move from the Trask ranch to Salinas, finally leaves for San Francisco to begin life anew as the owner of a bookstore. He leaves the boys money for food at the basketball game, and refuses Adam's offer of a ride to the train station. The boys, both flourishing at their new school, don't seem to even notice his absence, despite the fact that Lee has acted as both mother and father to them for their whole life. However, the twins are convinced of Lee's absolute love for them, and know full well that he will return shortly. Sure enough, six days later he returns and lets himself in to the house in Salinas, feeling for the first time ever in his life that he is finally home. No longer does he want a bookstore in San Francisco. He informs Adam that he feels "overwhelmingly glad to be home" with him, Cal, and Aron.

Cal and Aron attend the West End School in Salinas. At first they are intimidated by its size, but since they are both bright students, they soon become acclimated to life in the seventh grade. It short time, it becomes apparent to the other students that although they are twins, they possess very different personalities. Although Cal has no friends: "everyone was touched with fear of him and through fear with respect," and he quickly becomes a leader. Aron is far more fragile and shy, but very capable of defending himself physically. He quickly makes many friends, unlike his brother. Aron is still smitten with Abra Bacon, who returns his attentions. The children, who fell in love upon first meeting, talk of marriage, and call each other husband and wife. One day, Aron talks about his mother and puts his head in Abra's lap. At the first expression of maternal attention that the youngster has ever experienced, Aron breaks into tears, and Abra comforts him with a tenderness that speaks to the woman she will turn out to be. They talk of Aron's mother, and Abra intimates that she had heard rumors about Kate living in Salinas. He refuses to deal with this possibility, but after Abra leaves he returns to the shady grove they shared and thinks about the possibility that his mother might still be alive. He is psychologically distraught: how could it be possible that his father lied to him? He refuses to even think of such a possibility, and rejects the idea of his mother's existence in Salinas. "He pushe[s] his mother back into death," and returns to the safety of his home, and the love of Adam and Lee.

Time goes on: Lee begins to spend money furnishing the Trask house, even buying an icebox. For some inexplicable reason, Adam is enthralled with the invention, and decides to invest most of his fortune in preserving food through refrigeration. By now World War I has broken out, and Adam devises a plan to transport lettuce by rail from California to the East Coast during the winter. The whole town celebrates the departure of the train, but everyone laughs uproariously when they find out that only wet, soggy garbage arrived in New York. In short, the venture is disastrous, and Adam must live with the ridicule of the townspeople. Furthermore, his inheritance has dwindled to $9.000. Cal and Aron also become objects of ridicule, and are called "lettuceheads". Cal is able to laugh off the lessening of his social position, but Aron remains angry with his father and feels mortified. Abra attempts to temper his rage to no avail, and reasserts her belief that Aron should ask his father point–blank about his mother's death. Aron runs away from her, and Abra feels lonely and saddened by his actions. Cal also feels lonely and jealous of the bond between Aron and Abra. He attempts at one point to attract Abra, but she rebuffs him, and he continues to walk the streets at night in pain and solitude: "always there was the darkness about him."

Analysis

Steinbeck insists that when a new land is being developed, strong individuals (like those who make up the initial wave of immigrants) arrive first. They perform the back–breaking work, clearing the land and establishing the basic structures of society, before being followed by industrialists and bankers, and finally by lawyers, who are in – at least in Steinbeck's estimation – weaker specimens of mankind. As examples of the strong workers who establish the foundations of society, Steinbeck cites Samuel and Liza Hamilton. After leaving Ireland, their homeland, they had to travel to California where, for financial reasons, they were forced to settle on the most barren land in the Salinas Valley, eking out a living from sun–up to sun–down. It was the couple's strength, fortitude, grace, and love that enabled them to successfully feed and raise nine children. However, many of their children seem like mere copies of the originals, with only a single generation's removal making them far weaker than their parents. For instance, while Samuel and Liza work hard and survive admirably on the driest land in the Valley, their children, Tom and Dessie, are merely watered–down versions of their parents. Sameul and Liza's offspring simply lack the strength to survive the vicissitudes of the world, even though it could be argued that they have far easier lives than their parents. Tom is not even close to being on a par with his father both mentally and physically, and Dessie succumbs early on to a weak body, unlike her physically strong mother. While their brother Will, the car salesman and business entrepreneur, certainly possesses the wherewithal to succeed, he lacks his father's impeccable sense of honesty.

Time moves on, and as the older generation declines, a change in tone occurs in the novel: gradually, the author becomes more and more concerned with the omnipresence of death. Indeed, seven characters have died already: Samuel, Liza, Una, Tom, and Dessie Hamilton, Charles Trask, and Lee's mother. The automobile that Adam buys after attending Samuel Hamilton's funeral and the closing of Dessie Hamilton's dress–making business illustrates the changing times and the effects that the advance of automation has on individuals. It is important to note that Steinbeck completed this novel when he was 62 years old himself, and that many scholars have maintained that *East of Eden* was the author's final opportunity to offer parting words of wisdom to younger generations. In this section of the novel, Steinbeck preaches about the sacredness of truth and the privilege of being able to choose good over evil.

Many of Steinbeck's characters lie to protect those whom they love. Samuel lies to Adam about his wife's whereabouts to protect him from the psychological pain of finding out that she is a notorious whore and brothel owner. In turn, Adam lies to the twins and tells them that their mother is dead, again to protect them from knowing the truth – that their mother abandoned them when they were a week old. Cal continues the family tradition of dishonesty by failing to acknowledge to Adam and Lee that he has found out the truth, and by continuing to lie to his brother, Aron, in an effort to protect him. Dessie lies to her brother Tom about her stomach problems to keep him from being hurt, and he lies about his own psychological malady to spare his sister. Despite his better judgment, Lee keeps the family secret, but attempts to persuade Adam to tell his sons the truth before they find out about their mother from others. In his effort to get Adam to tell the truth to the boys, Lee shares the horrific story about his mother, thereby conveying his belief that while his father could have chosen to keep the truth about his birth a secret, he chose not to spare his son out of respect. It was, after all, Lee's life, and he deserved to know the particulars. Lee insists that Adam should likewise inform the boys of their true beginnings.

At this point in the novel, Aron and Cal become central to the plot. Once more, the Cain and Abel paradigm unfolds, with Cal continuing in the dark Cain role, and Aron, the golden boy, taking the place of Abel. Cal, however, is soon revealed as the protagonist, despite the reader's expectations that Aron will assume the leading role. Initially, the mild–mannered Aron shines, while Cal is removed from the action. Aron immediately puts Abra on a very high pedestal, as Adam once – very erroneously – did to Cathy. Aron, however, remains static throughout the novel. He is predictable from the start: he never grows as a character, while Cal becomes far more introspective and real. At this point, Aron begins to act as a foil for Cal. He is loved and admired by all ,while Cal finds himself without friends. Inversely, however, we see that Aron cannot accept his father's business losses: he is personally humiliated, and never thinks about how this embarrassing financial fiasco might be affecting his father or other members of the family. Here, Steinbeck foreshadows Aron's later behavior. Cal, on the other hand, is deeply sorry for his father's losses. In short, it appears that Cal loves his father more than Aron does, while Adam loves Aron more than Cal. This is precisely the familial dynamic that caused Charles to strike out in jealousy against his brother, Adam, who was favored by their father, Cyrus.

Summary and Analysis of Chapters 38–45

As Cal becomes older his restlessness increases, and he begins wandering the streets of Salinas at night, wondering why everyone has lied to him about his mother. When a drunk named Rabbit Holman (who doesn't know Cal's identity) invites him to Kate's brothel after informing him that the owner is Adam Trask's wife, who shot her husband in the arm, Cal is confronted with the truth about his mother. Young Cal is stunned – to put it mildly – and runs to Lee for an explanation. Cal is extremely worried that he has inherited his mother's evil nature: "I hate her because...I've got her in me." Lee soothes the confused teen by assuring him that he can choose goodness over evil at any time. Cal realizes how much he loves his father, and his desire for Adam to return that love increases. In marked contrast to Cal, Aron moves ever deeper into religion. He joins the Episcopal Church and tells Abra (who is none to happy about these developments) that he plans on living a life of celibacy. Cal, whom Aron has labeled a sinner, thinks about telling Aron about his mother to get him off his high horse, but refrains because he believes that Aron is too psychologically vulnerable to endure the pain of this revelation. While his brother prays, Cal continues his nighttime wanderings. One night, he is arrested during a police raid, and Adam comes to bail him out. For the first time, Adam tells his mortified son about his sojourns in jail as a young man. Cal is amazed to learn that his father spent time on a chain gang. Cal then tells Adam what he knows about Kate, and both agree to continue to keep the truth from Aron.

However, Cal cannot get his mother out of his mind, and begins to stalk her "to learn all he could about her." He waits outside the brothel and follows her on her errands, and even arranges his classes to accommodate her schedule. One day, Kate notices that someone is following her and confronts the stranger, only to discover that it is her son, Cal. Inside the whorehouse, she takes him into her "gray room", explaining that she stays in the dark room because the light hurts her eyes. Cal notices that her hands are gnarled from severe arthritis. After inquiring about Aron, Kate begins to mock Cal's father, but Cal refuses to listen to her slander. She tells Cal that she believes that he and she are very much alike: "you're my kind. Maybe you're the same." The idea horrifies Cal until he recalls Lee's contention that all humans have free choice. He does not have to be like his mother. He tells her that he was once afraid that he was indeed like her, but that he is no longer worried. Call then tells her that he believes that she doesn't live in the gray room because of her eyes, but because she is afraid. At this point, Kate becomes angry. Unable to stand being called weak, she tells him to leave. "I'm going," he says, "but I'm glad you're afraid." After he leaves, Kate looks down at the vial of morphine that hangs around her neck. Cal hit a bulls–eye when he told her that she lived in fear. At this point, Steinbeck reiterates how Kate has been living since learning about Charles Trask's inheritance. Shortly after she took the money, she began to be troubled by arthritis pains. She was also disturbed by a visit from Ethel, a prostitute who used to work for Faye. Ethyl told Kate that she had the empty bottles of poison that she had buried after killing

Faye, and attempted to blackmail her for $100 a month. In a panic, Kate has Ethyl arrested and ordered to leave town, but she becomes increasingly paranoid that Ethyl might tell someone else about Faye's unnatural demise. Worried that her actions might come back to haunt her, Kate decides to save even more money so that she can move to New York. She retreats into her gray room and rarely leaves the building. When she realizes that a stranger – Cal – is following her, she becomes even more distraught.

As World War I approaches, Cal suggests that he and Aron leave school and return to the family ranch to earn money. Cal wants to help his father, but Aron wants to leave Salinas and go away to college because he still feels humiliated by his father's failed business venture. However, Aron is afraid that his father might not have the money for the tuition at Stanford, the school he wishes to attend. The ever–practical Cal convinces Aron to take extra classes and graduate from high school a year early so that he can go to college sooner. Lee offers Cal his life savings of $5,000 to help finance a business venture. Although he is still a teenager, Cal demonstrates a strong sense of business acumen by going to see Will Hamilton. He forms a partnership with the wealthy son of Samuel Hamilton to market beans during the upcoming war. Their plan is to guarantee the Salinas farmers five cents per pound of beans (instead of the 3.5 cents they presently receive), and then sell the beans overseas at a tremendous profit after the war breaks out. However, World War I doesn't seem real to the town of Salinas, and it isn't "until the dreadful telegrams began to sneak sorrowfully in" that the town comes to realize the real impact of war. Steinbeck underscores the incongruity of being 6,000 miles from the noise of war, yet feeling the agony of losing loved ones nonetheless. No mention is made here of the effect of the war on the Trask family, which has two draft–age sons.

Adam feels inordinately proud of Aron's academic successes, especially when he learns that he is secretly working hard to finish high school a year early. He tells Lee, "I'm proud of him. Terribly proud," and says how much he wishes that Cal could show the same academic inclinations. Maybe, he says wistfully, Cal is also secretly working on something wonderful. Adam clearly favors Aron over his other son, to Cal's great consternation. Aron spends much of his time studying with Mr. Rolf, an Episcopal minister who comes to have great influence over him. When Aron does indeed pass his college entrance examinations a year early, he fails to tell his father, who has a gold watch waiting for the graduation announcement. All Aron can think about is getting away from this "dirty town": "I want to go away," he tells Lee, who responds that "things are neither so good nor so bad as they seem to you now." Lee advises him that if he pretends that everything is fine and goes through the motions of living well, things just might become better in time. Then Lee tells Aron that his father has left a graduation gift for him under his pillow.

After Adam goes off to Stanford, he finds – to his great consternation – that college is nothing like he expected. Desperately homesick, he writes letters to Abra full of love and promises, but has no interactions with the other students. In his absence, Abra visits more and more with the Trasks, and in short time becomes almost a member of the family. She becomes particularly close to Lee, and tells him all about her family. When she asks Lee about Aron and Cal's mother, Lee tells her the truth. Abra also voices her concern about Aron's false impression of her. She insists that she is just a normal human being with both good and bad characteristics, and worries that she will never be able to live up to Aron's expectations. She feels that he thinks of her as far too pure, and doesn't see who she really is.

While Aron is living in a religious fantasy, Cal finds himself solidly enmeshed in the real adult world. He pays back Lee's original $5,000 loan and plans to tell his father of his successful business venture on Thanksgiving, when he plans to give Adam a gift of $15,000 to restore the family's financial losses. He talks with Abra, who confides in him that she is not as perfect as his brother thinks she is. Cal, however, doesn't take her seriously.

Simultaneously, things are heating up on the other side of town, at Kate's brothel. Kate's bodyguard, the escaped San Quentin convict Joe Valery (who works at the whorehouse as a pimp) is sent by Kate to track down Ethyl. Her paranoia has continued to escalate, and she can no longer contain her anxiety about the possibility that Ethyl might be speaking to others about the circumstances of Faye's death. The ruthless and savage Joe has taken over more and more of the responsibilities at the brothel, as Kate's arthritic hands keep her from being too active. He realizes that Kate is losing her mind, and sees this as an opportunity to get more money out of her. Kate, however, mistakenly believes that she can control him, and offers him $500 to find and dispose of Ethyl. After wandering around the nearby towns of Monterey, Watsonville, and Santa Cruz, Joe learns that Ethyl has drowned, but tells Kate that she is alive and planning to return to Salinas. Kate has since seen her angelic–looking son Aron from a distance, and has been feeling much better, having even begun dreaming of moving to New York, establishing herself as a respectable woman, and having her son come to visit. The news about Ethyl, however, throws her even deeper into her paranoia, and she locks herself in her gray room. Joe sees how much his news disturbs Kate, and erroneously comes to believe that he is gaining power over her.

Analysis

Ever since their birth, it has appeared as though the devout, angelic–looking Aron is destined to do good, while the darker Cal is fated to be evil. The natural assumption is that the Cain and Abel story will play out in this generation as well, with Cal murdering – or at least harming – his brother in a jealous rage. However, this black–and–white proposition takes on shades of gray as the twins approach adulthood. Indeed, Aron seems to be out of touch with reality, and as he sinks deeper and deeper into religious fanaticism, his innate selfishness reveals itself. He scorns his father and continues to feel great shame over the family's financial losses even after he reaches an age when he should be able to understand the realities of the business world. Although he is angry with his father, he nevertheless runs away to school and allows Adam to support him. He idealizes Abra, but never takes the time to get to know her as a human being. He puts her on an impossibly high pedestal, yet fails to consider her desires when he announces his plans to live a life of celibacy.

Unlike Aron, Cal seems to be evolving into a responsible, caring adult. He supports his brother throughout high school, and continues to help pay for his college tuition. He saves money so his father can regain his financial standing (even though it is worth noting that he earns the money by taking advantage of the need for food during wartime). Although he is attracted to Abra, Cal respects the fact that she is his brother's girlfriend. He also treats Lee with great consideration and kindness. Cal spends his nights wandering the town, gambling, and seeing prostitutes, but this behavior causes him great concern. Even though Cal is cast in the dark role of the biblical Cain, he struggles to become a better, more moral person. He loves his family, and displays a strong sense of intuition in recognizing the deadening fear that lies behind Cathy's brusque behavior. Indeed, he has an aptitude for understanding the intricacies of evil and goodness – a trait that Abra later comes to admire. Eventually, she falls in love with Cal, preferring his realistic view of her to Aron's idealization. Here, Steinbeck returns to the concept of *timshel*, or free will: Aron remains a deluded, ill–tempered child, while Cal struggles to become a better man.

In this section, Steinbeck also juxtaposes Aron with Adam. Father and son are remarkably alike, and are an apt demonstration of how family history is oftentimes repeated. At the beginning of the novel, it becomes clear that Adam hates his father, Cyrus. Similarly, near the end of the novel we learn that Aron hates *his* father, Adam. Even so, both fathers love the son that does not return their affections more than the son that adores them. Cyrus loved his older son, Adam, more that he did his younger son, Charles, as was evidenced by his preference of Aron's gift of a mongrel puppy over Charles' gift of an expensive knife. Charles, he believed, had a dark nature, and Cyrus kept him at a distance instead of attempting to find out how he could help his unhappy son. Similarly, Adam adores Aron, while Aron despises his father for no good reason. Aron is in fact cruel to his father, and runs away to school simply to get away from him. Adam turns a blind eye to this treatment, as he once did to his wife, Cathy. Indeed, Adam's feelings for Cathy seem to be the root of this preference. In time, Cal comes to realize that Adam favors Aron because of his physical resemblance to their mother. Adam is also blind to the affections of Cal, the son who loves him more than anyone else on earth, and fails to recognize all that his son is doing to help him. This tension continues to surface in the last part of the novel; once more, family history repeats itself when Cal gives Adam the $15,000 he earned to restore his father's fortune.

Although Steinbeck primarily focuses on his male characters, he draws a comparison between two important female characters: Cathy and Abra. Early on, Adam viewed Cathy as innocent and pure, and his son Aron views Abra in a similar light. He places her on such a high pedestal that she has nowhere to go but down. Cathy and Abra must therefore be viewed through the same lens. If Aron and Adam are so similar, can Abra and Cathy really be so different? In other words, is it possible that Abra might turn away from her inherent goodness and embrace her dark side? Abra fears this possibility more than anything, even asking Lee about her evil impulses. She feels that Aron holds her in far too high regard, and tells Cal that she is not as pure as she seems. The discovery that Abra's father is a thief only escalates her worries in this regard. However, an analysis of the two women as children reveals their inherent differences: Cathy never once did a good thing for anyone, while Abra was a sweet child who demonstrated an early maternal tenderness, comforting Aron when he needed her most. Abra, like Cal, recognizes that all humans have impulses towards evil, but that each individual has the ability to choose to live a good, moral life.

Summary and Analysis of Chapters 46–54

World War I changes the town of Salinas into a busy beehive. Everyone is wrapped up in a patriotic fervor, selling war bonds or rolling bandages: "There were people who gave everything they had to the war because it was the last war and by winning it we would remove war like a thorn from the flesh of the world." Even the children are affected: Steinbeck shares an autobiographical incident in which he and his sister taunted a German gentleman named Mr. Fenchel. As chairman of the draft board, Adam suffers excruciating guilt over the responsibility of sending young men off to war. Indeed, he feels "like a hanging judge who hates the gallows." Adam has, after all, experienced such fighting himself, and has come to view war as a "reversal of the rules where a man is permitted to kill all the humans he can." When Adam talks to Lee about the horror involved in his job as chairman of the draft board, Lee tells him that he has a choice in the matter. Adam, however, feels compelled to do what he sees as his duty to his country. Meanwhile, the whole Trask family awaits Aron's return from Stanford at Thanksgiving. Adam has come to believe that Aron might be smarter than Cal, and has a party planned to demonstrate to Aron how happy he is with his academic efforts. Meanwhile, completely unbeknownst to his family, Aron is miserable at school: he has no friends, and is virtually ignored by his classmates. He has sunk into a pit of despair that goes beyond depression, and counts down the days until he can return home to his family and his beloved, Abra. Unhappy with everything about Stanford, he decides that he will not ever return to the school.

While Aron suffers at Stanford, Kate has become suspicious of Joe Valery's continued attempts to extort money from her. She becomes more and more incapacitated by her arthritis, and considers committing suicide by ingesting the morphine that she carries in a vial around her neck. Valery thinks about how drastically the tables have turned, and fantasizes about how he will soon totally control her and have complete run of the brothel. He sees Kate's obsession with Ethyl as the means to this end. Kate, however, has an instinct for deceit, and knows that Joe is lying to her. She tells him that she's had a change of heart about Ethyl, and that she doesn't want the old prostitute dead after all. She explains to Joe that she believed Ethyl had done her a disservice in the past, but that in retrospect she as come to realize that she has treated Ethyl unfairly. Kate tells Joe that she now wants him to bring Ethyl to her, saying, "she didn't do anything to me." Kate, however, is barely holding herself together, and has begun constantly fingering the vial of morphine hanging around her neck. Her paranoia escalates even further when she considers the possibility of another visit from Ethyl. The idea of suicide brings her the only form of respite left in her life. Never will she know the comfort that could be provided by her children, Aron and Cal Trask.

Aron Trask arrives home for Thanksgiving, to the enormous delight of his family. However, he is put off by the overwhelming attentions of his father and Adam's ambitious plans for his future. He fails to tell Adam that he does not even want to return to Stanford. Cal, jealous about the fuss being made over Aron, gift–wraps the $15,000 that he plans to give his father in gold certificates, fully aware that he is making the enormously generous gift in an attempt to buy his father's love ("I'm trying to buy him"). However, he realizes that Adam loves Aron more because Aron resembles his mother, Cathy: "it's because he looks like her. My father never got over her." He seems to hope that his generous gift will win him a small portion of his father's heart. However, Cal is devastated when Adam opens the certificates and rebukes him instead of kissing him. Adam angrily accuses Cal of stealing money from vulnerable people in need of food during the war. He tells Cal that he doesn't want the money, and that he would have been much happier if he had gone to college and made him proud, as Aron did. Almost in tears, Cal rushes from the room. Lee counsels him to control his anger and to remember that his free will can help him to make proper choices. A short while later he apologizes to Adam, but doesn't seem sincere. He seeks out the company of his brother, Aron, and tells him that he has something he wants to show him. Cal leads Aron toward Castroville Street, the site of their mother's whorehouse, and Aron comes to finally realize the full truth about his mother. Horrified, Aron runs away and joins the army.

On the same day that her son enlists, Kate's silence is making Joe Valery extremely uncomfortable. He believes that Kate, who has cloistered herself in her gray room, is plotting against him, but Kate is instead reacting to the events of the previous evening, when Cal brought Aron to the brothel: "she saw the face of the blond and beautiful boy, his eyes mad with shock." She then recalls her other son, the dark–haired Cal, "leaning against the door and laughing." Why, she wonders, would Cal have done such a thing to his brother? At this point, she recalls a traumatic childhood incident: as a little girl of about five, she grew fearful of all the adults surrounding her because they seemed to be as tall as trees. She sought refuge from this fear in the novel *Alice in Wonderland*, in which the young protagonist grows so small that no one can see her. Kate begins to cry, and for the fist time in her life becomes aware that she is missing some innate human quality. She deduces that Joe has been lying to her about Ethyl, and develops a plan. First, she calls the sheriff to tell him about Joe Valery. She then sits down and writes her will, in which she leaves all of her belongings to Aron. Next, she administers a fatal does of the morphine that she has kept in a vial around her neck for this purpose, and sits down to die, all the while reliving the childhood fantasy of *Alice in Wonderland*. The next morning, after finding Kate's dead body, Joe is riffling through her papers when he discovers photographs of Kate's customers, some of the town's most prominent men, in compromising sexual positions, along with a safe deposit key and her handwritten will. Joe is euphoric, believing that he has hit pay dirt for the first time ever in his life. He believes that he will be able to open the safe deposit box, and will make a fortune blackmailing the men in the photographs. He doesn't have time to act, however, because a deputy, having been tipped off by Kate's note to Sheriff Horace Quinn, arrives and shoots him when he tries to escape.

The former deputy, Sheriff Horace Quinn, rummages through the photographs that Kate intended to use to blackmail the town's prominent men and burns them in front of a lawyer, who agrees to let the men in question know that the evidence against them has been destroyed. He realizes, however, that this action will most likely result in the loss of his job, because the important men in the photographs will know that he is aware of their aberrant behavior. The sheriff then visits Adam to tell him about Kate's suicide, and to let him know that his son Aron is his mother's sole beneficiary, having been left $100,000. Adam is emotionally shattered and cries out "Oh, my poor darling." The sheriff insists that Aron be told the truth, even though Adam requests that he not inform Aron about his mother's will. Adam does not yet realize that Aron already knows the truth about his mother, nor does he know that Aron has run away and joined the army. Aron has been missing for two nights. When Cal is questioned about Aron's whereabouts, he sarcastically replies, "Am I supposed to look after him?" Adam's health begins to fail, and he finds solace in the belief that Aron has merely returned to Stanford. In search of comfort, Lee reads from *The Meditations of Marcus Aurelius*, a book he once stole from Samuel Hamilton. The text reveals to him that he will die soon, and yet he has not found peace.

After experiencing momentary joy from having avenged himself at the whorehouse, Cal sinks into despair. He begins to drink heavily in a desperate attempt to alleviate his guilt, but knows that the only way he will be able to find any modicum of comfort is if he confesses his actions to his father and begs his forgiveness. He doesn't know yet that Aron has enlisted in the army, and desperately hopes that he will return home soon. In the company of Lee, he makes a sacrificial offering by burning the $15,000 that his father so adamantly rejected. Lee, however, doesn't let Cal off this lightly. He lectures him against seeking revenge, but says that he now must pull himself out of the pit of despair into which he has slipped. He explains to the young man that we are all human, made up of both good and bad characteristics, and that we all make mistakes that can be rectified. "We are all," Lee explains, "descended from the restless, the nervous, the criminals, the arguers and brawlers, but also the brave and independent and generous." Cal feels better after their discussion, and tries not to beat himself up any longer. Shortly after his talk with Cal, Lee finds Adam standing just inside the front door, in a state of shock: he has just received a post card from Aron informing him that he has lied about his age to enlist in the army. Adam, who has suffered a stroke, continues to decline. He cannot move his limbs very well, and his eyesight is diminished. Why, he wonders, would Aron have enlisted in the army? Cal is torn between telling his father the truth, and sparing him the pain of knowledge. Lee believes that Cal should wait until Adam's health improves, and prompts him to bring Abra for a visit. Abra tells Cal that she has received a card from Aron telling her that he doesn't feel clean anymore, and that she should forget about him. Cal tells Abra about taking Aron to Kate's house on Thanksgiving, and Abra reveals to Cal that she has known about Kate all along. She also tells Cal that she doesn't love Aron, and hasn't for some time. He has never grown up, she says. She then tells Cal that she loves him, not Aron. Shortly afterward, she explains to Cal that her father is a thief. Relieved by these revelations, she burns Aron's card.

Adam begins sleeping more and more. One day, during an introspective conversation with Lee about a dream, Adam reminisces about the fortune left to him by his father, Cyrus Trask: "he was a thief," he says. Lee immediately sees the hypocrisy involved in the idea of the deeply honest Adam Trask living off an ill–gained fortune. He contemplates how much Samuel Hamilton would enjoy the symmetry of Aron choosing to live off the profits of his mother's whorehouse. Abra visits the Trask household, and Lee is particularly glad to see her. He tells her that he wishes she was his daughter, and she acknowledges her deep, fatherly love for him. He gives Abra his mother's jade ornament, her only possession. The young girl is deeply moved and tenderly kisses the old man, the first kiss Lee has ever received. She tells Lee about burning Aron's letters, and how free she feels now that she has rejected Aron's idealized image of her. Intuiting her feelings about Cal, Lee tells Abra that he is a young man full of both good and bad.

Cal and Abra walk home together, discussing their plan to look for azaleas as soon as spring arrives. Their relationship deepens, and Cal decides to place flowers on his mother's grave: "I'm beginning to think like Aron," he tells himself. His father's health starts to improve. Word spreads that the azaleas are in bloom, and Cal and Abra go on a picnic by a stream. Although Cal is apprehensive, Abra holds his hand and tells him the truth about her father's criminal past. Meanwhile, at the quiet Trask house, Lee is filled with dread as he sits turning the pages of a spring seed catalog. In the silence of the house, he thinks a ghost is present. The doorbell rings, and Lee opens the door to find a man delivering a telegram: Aron has been killed in the war. Initially, he feels anger toward Aron for having left his family, and calls him a coward while he prepares medication for Adam. When Adam returns home, Lee, always an advocate of the truth, tells him that his son is dead, and Adam suffers a massive stroke. He might live for a couple of years, or "he might die tonight," Dr. Murphy says.

Cal returns to find his father near death, and sits down by his bed. "I'm responsible for Aron's death," he tells his father, although he is unsure whether he can understand him. "I took him to Kate's. I showed him his mother." Lee finds the youngster completely distraught: "I killed my brother. I'm a murderer," he cries out. Lee attempts to soothe him and tells him to go get Abra. Over glasses of liquor, Lee tells them both that they are in control of their own lives, and that they do not have to live in emulation of their sinful parents. Cal, Abra, and Lee stand before Adam as he lies on his death bed. Lee explains that Cal has done something that has resulted in Aron's death and Adam's stroke, and that he is experiencing overwhelming guilt. Then, he asks Adam to bless his son. Finally understanding how much Cal loves him, Adam raises his hand and blesses his son with the final word of the novel, *timshel*, before closing his eyes.

Analysis

The exchange of gifts is an important motif throughout *East of Eden*: these exchanges often inspire change and provide insights into individual characters. From the beginning, Cyrus Trask's preference of Adam's gift of a puppy over Charles' gift of an expensive knife sets up the central tension in the novel: the jealousy between brothers. This, of course, parallels God's rejection of Cain's gift in favor of Abel's. Similarly, Adam's rejection of Cal's gift of $15,000 parallels his own father's rejection of Charles' gift at the beginning of the novel. Readers are left wondering whether anyone ever truly learns, which is precisely Steinbeck's intent: mankind as a whole, he believes, never does learn, although individuals might.

The exchange of gifts occurs between other characters as well. After his death, Cyrus passes along a gift of $100,000 to his sons who, despite knowing that the money is ill–gained, accept the cash regardless. This undoubtedly casts a shadow over Charles – which, given his dark nature, is hardly surprising – but also casts Adam in a negative light. Upon his own death, Charles passes along the same amount, $100,000, to be divided between Adam and his wife, Kate. Unsurprisingly, Kate takes the money, but once more Adam accepts money which was gained at a cost to others. He fails to take this opportunity to expiate his guilt. Once again, he is cast as a less–than–palatable character – in fact, his reaction to Cal's gift can be viewed as downright hypocritical. Although Adam righteously feels that he cannot accept his son's gift, he fails to comprehend the pure gesture of love that lies behind the impulse. He cannot see that he himself has never held a job, and has lived off his father's and brother's stolen money for years. In the last section of the novel, Kate leaves her son Aron the same gift of $100,000, in effect passing along the sins of the fathers and the mothers. Readers are, however, prevented from learning whether or not the deeply religious Aron could or would have accepted money made from prostitution. Furthermore, we can only hypothesize whether or not Cal will accept his father and brother's ill–gained money after their deaths. Once again, Cal will be offered the choice between right and wrong.

It is important to consider why Kate left all of her money to Aron, a boy she earlier showed absolutely no regard for, and who only came to her attention after his brother, Cal, came to see her. She sees Aron in church and becomes smitten with him, and returns to watch him again and again, although he doesn't even know of her existence. After Aron shows up at the brothel, Kate is overwrought and commits suicide, leaving all her money to Aron. We can only speculate that Cal will be unwilling to accept his father and brother's ill–gained money, given the fact that he earlier burned the $15,000 he had been planning to give to his father as a sacrificial offering. Not all gifts in the novel, however, have strings attached. For example, Lee's gift of his mother's jade brooch to Abra is a gesture of pure love.

Abra's presence is heightened towards the end of the novel. She says that she is often bad, but readers never see her as anything but caring and loving. In short, Abra provides balance in a novel that has been frequently criticized for its highly negative portrayal of women. Indeed, Cathy Trask is one of the most notable evil female characters in American literature. Cathy is portrayed as the devil incarnate: she is often likened to a cat, prefers to live in the dark, has small, sharp teeth, and scratches and bits those who offend her. Even her name, Cathy, recalls the word "cat", and she runs away, as cats are wont to do. Abra, on the other hand, is caring and maternal, and quickly becomes a dear member of the Trask family. She demonstrates her introspective nature when she becomes worried that she will inherit her father's propensity for evil. She loves Lee deeply (in contrast to Cathy, who hates Lee), and is the only person ever to kiss him. By marrying Abra, Cal increases his chances of successfully utilizing the novel's central concept of *timshel.*

Timshel is, simply put, the key to escaping the ongoing human battle between good and evil that rages throughout *East of Eden*. Believed to be the most important word in the world by Lee, it states unequivocally that each individual has been given the freedom by God to overcome evil if they make the choice to do good. The Cain and Abel fable plays out in the conclusion of the novel, when Aron dies. After he kills his brother Abel, Cain is told by God that although he will face exile as punishment, he has the freedom to choose to do good over evil. In effect, Cain (Cal) has once again "killed" his brother Abel (Aron). However, Aron was killed because he ran away to join the army: while it might seem that Cal caused his death, it was Aron's free will determined his own end. Unlike Lee, Cathy believes that humanity is inherently evil, and lashes out at the world in her attempt to prove herself correct. She photographs prominent men in sexually compromising situations and leads others into sexually deviant behavior, believing that all humans are wholly evil. She never once considers the possibility that sexual deviance might be their only flaw. She commits suicide after encountering her son, Aron. It is possible that Aron, who wanted to see only goodness and perfection in the world, was too threatening to Kate's sense of self.

Aron also is at fault: he goes to the other extreme by accepting only the good in people. He views Abra as a saint, completely ignoring the fact that she, like every human, has negative qualities as well. Cal, on the other hand, represents the middle ground. He struggles to be good, but knows full well that he sometimes performs poorly in this regard. However, Cal is aware of when he is bad. His guilty feelings in the wake of Aron's death inspire him to change. Ultimately, with the counseling of the wise philosopher, Lee, he is successful. By the end of the novel, he has come to realize that he can ask for forgiveness and choose to behave better in the future. He realizes that all human beings are fragile and imperfect, that they all commit sins, and that the concept of *timshel* offers hope for a better future. The sins of the fathers do not have to be visited upon the sons. The sons – and the daughters, for that matter – can make better choices in the ongoing struggle between good and evil.

Steinbeck believed that the battle between good and evil dominates all of human history. Since the time of Adam and Eve, humans have struggled with their evil impulses and desire to do good. Throughout the novel, Steinbeck reiterates over and over that man as a whole will never learn to overcome evil, but that individuals have the ability to make good decisions. Ultimately, *East of Eden* has a positive ending: Cal and Abra both come to realize that they are not doomed to repeat the mistakes of their parents. Cal's worries that he has inherited Cathy's evil nature, it appears, will not come to fruition. Abra will most likely not be a thief like her father. Both will be better parents then their own parents were, because Lee has helped them to see that they have the choice to select good over evil.

Suggested Essay Questions

1. The Chinese–American character Lee is a philosopher who first brings the novel's central theme to light for Samuel Hamilton and Adam Trask. Discuss Lee's role in the novel. What are his contributions?
2. The novel opens with a vision of California's Salinas Valley. How does Steinbeck use landscape to illustrate the novel's major themes?
3. Cyrus Trask and Samuel Hamilton portray archtypcal, albeit very different, father–figures. Discuss fatherhood in *East of Eden*, illustrating the importance of each type of father–figure.
4. The Trask Family and the Hamilton Family make up most of the characters in the novel. Discuss the intrinsic nature of each family and how their differing dynamics affect the outcome of the novel.
5. Cathy Ames has been criticized by scholars as "unbelievable" because she is wholly evil. Do you agree, or disagree? What is Cathy's significance in the novel?
6. The biblical story of Cain and Abel plays a crucial role in the novel. Discuss the intergenerational significance of this story.
7. The concept of *timshel* ("thou mayest") is central to the novel. Discuss this idea and its pertinence to the novel.
8. Although he is not the protagonist, Samuel Hamilton deeply influences the events that take place in the novel. What is his significance in *East of Eden*?
9. Steinbeck's female characters have been criticized by scholars as being "unreal": far too good, or far too evil. Select four female characters and argue for or against this point.
10. Discuss the similarities and differences between the two sets of brothers (Charles and Adam, and Cal and Aron), paying particular attention to the end of the novel.

Cain and Abel

The biblical story of Cain and Abel plays a central role in the novel *East of Eden*. In "Genesis", Adam and Eve's sons, Cain and Abel, offer sacrifices to God. The shepherd Abel sacrifices his best lamb, while the farmer Cain offers grain. Because God prefers Abel's gift over Cain's, Cain becomes infuriated and kills his brother in a jealous rage. When God inquires into Abel's whereabouts, Cain retorts, "Am I my brother's keeper?" God tells him that his brother's blood cries out to him from the ground, and that he is cursed. God marks Cain, and banishes him to wander the earth.

The characters of Charles and Adam Trask (who share the initials CAwith their biblical forebears) closely follow the Cain and Abel paradigm. Cyrus Trask favors Adam's birthday gift of a puppy over Charles' gift of an expensive knife, and Charles almost beats his brother Adam to death in a jealous rage. However, unlike Charles (Cain), Adam (Abel) becomes the wanderer, first in the army, then as a vagabond, and then in South America. Finally, Adam moves to California, where he settles and raises his twin sons. His bitter brother remains on their Connecticut farm. One day he has a farm accident which results in a large facial scar, a mark akin to Cain's. When Charles dies, he leaves his fortune to his brother: clearly, although jealousy drove them apart, the brotherly bond is still there.

Years later, Adam's wife Cathy ("Kate") Trask gives birth to the next generation of Trask brothers, the dark–haired Caleb Trask (Cal) and the fair–haired Aron Trask – another set of brothers who share the initials C Unsurprisingly, these brothers perpetuate the Cain and Abel motif. After the birth of their sons, Cathy abandons Adam, and he sinks into such a severe depression that he neglects to even name his children. When Samuel Hamilton hears of this, he rushes to the Trask ranch and finds the children asleep on the warm ground (recalling God's declaration that Abel's blood cried out from the ground). Samuel suggests to Adam that he name the children Cain and Abel, but Adam won't hear of it.

Adam favors Aron over Cal, much as Cyrus preferred Charles over Adam and God preferred Abel over Cain. When Cal offers Adam a birthday present of $15,000, Adam berates him for having taken advantage of farmers during war–time. Unable to contain his jealousy, Cal takes Aron to their mother's brothel, destroying Aron's belief that Cathy is dead. Aron is completely devastated and joins the army, resulting in his death in France. The "Genesis" tale thus plays out in the Trask family, with Cal, albeit inadvertently, killing his brother.

Author of ClassicNote and Sources

Casey Diana, author of ClassicNote. Completed on January 25, 2006, copyright held by GradeSaver.

Updated and revised Jordan Berkow April 11, 2006. Copyright held by GradeSaver.

Beegel, Susan F. Steinbeck and the Environment: Interdisciplinary Approaches. Tuscaloosa, Alabama: University of Alabama Press, 1997.

DeMott, Robert J. Steinbeck's Typewriter: Essays on His Art. Troy, New York: Whitson Publishing Co., 1996.

Ditsky, John. John Steinbeck Life, Work and Criticism. Fredericton, Canada: York Press, 1985.

Owens, Louis. John Steinbeck's Re–Vision of America. Athens, Georgia: University of Georgia Press, 1985.

Shillinglaw, Susan and Kevin Hearle, eds. Beyond Boundaries: Rereading Steinbeck. Tuscaloosa, Alabama: University of Alabama Press, 2002.

Steinbeck, Elaine and Robert Wallsten. Steinbeck: A Life in Letters. London: Pan Books, 1979.

Steinbeck, John. Journal of a Novel: The East of Eden Letters. New York: Penguin Books, 1990.

Dickstein, Morris. "Steinbeck and the Great Depression." The South Atlantic Quarterly. 2004–01–01. 2006–01–10. <http://muse.jhu.edu>.

Meyer, Kenneth. "John Steinbeck's Promised Lands." Steinbeck Studies. 2004–01–01. 2006–01–09. <http://muse.jhu.edu.>.

Dickstein, Morris. "Steinbeck and the Great Depression." The South Atlantic Quarterly, 103 (2004): 111–131.

Ditsky, John. "I Kind of Like 'Caleb': Naming in East of Eden." Steinbeck Newsletter, 10 (1997): 7–9.

Lore, Craig M. "Abracadabra in Steinbeck's East of Eden." Steinbeck Newsletter, 10 (1997): 1.

Essay: Good and Evil in East of Eden

by Jaime Lynn Davis
August 21, 2000

In the novel East of Eden, Steinbeck emphasizes the theme of the struggle between good and evil. He says that this perpetual battle is the only true human story in that all of mankind can find themselves and their thoughts and actions in this tale. "We have only one story. All novels, all poetry, are built on the never–ending contest in ourselves of good and evil." Writers, musicians, farmers, and salesmen alike have found themselves caught in this internal conflict. Stein beck says, "I think this is the only story we have and that it occurs on all levels of feeling and intelligence." In East of Eden, many of the characters' struggles are obvious as they grow and learn of the often harsh and unjust world in which they were placed. Charles is torn between good and evil as a child faced with a father that only loves him second–best. Likewise, Cal feels that he is inferior to Aron's near perfection and must battle with himself constantly.

The story of good and evil, present throughout East of Eden, has been told since the beginning of mankind. In the Garden of Eden, man first became aware of the difference between virtue and vice after eating from the Tree of the Knowledge of Good and Evil. From that point on, humans had the choice to fall prey to sin or to rise about it and find God's favor. Since this story is common to each of us, it has been retold countless times in many different forms, from John Proctor's struggle in The Crucible to the creature's battle in Frankenstein. These stories and East of Eden have endured through the years because they tell the story of mankind and our never–ending quest to conquer evil with good.

In East of Eden, the struggle between good and evil is constantly seen both internally and between characters. Cathy, symbolizing Satan, looks for the evil in each person and tries to draw it out and exploit it. Steinbeck says, "And it occurs to me that evil must constantly respawn, while good, while virtue, is immortal. Vice has always a fresh young face, while virtue is venerable as nothing else in the world is." Cathy must change her name and appearance and move often to continue her corrupt work. After murdering her parents, she becomes Catherine Amesbury and later changes her name again to Kate after shooting Adam and leaving her sons. Cathy has to put on different faces regularly. To Faye, she is the sweet, adoring daughter, but to the girls who live in her whorehouse, she is the merciless punishment enforcer. She must constantly watch her steps and plan any action from start to finish to make sure she will be able to carry it out. This is the story of evil. Satan can always conceive new and creative ways to lure people to him and yet the evil always dies and is forgotten. On the other hand, virtue is remembered and honored from generation to generation. Samuel's teachings and philosophies are often relied on long after his death. Lee incorporates Samuel's teachings into his upraising of the Trask twins. Therefore, good always conquers in the end as it does in East of Eden. Cathy begins to realize reluctantly near the end of her life that the evil on which she thrived caused her downfall. She had trained herself never to trust anyone and in the end Cathy even began to doubt herself.

The most obvious case of an internal struggle between good and evil is present in Cal. As a child, he is aware that his light–haired brother is favored over him by nearly everyone. When Cal finally confronts his mother, he believes that Adam loves Aron more because he looks like Cathy. Cal's peers are scared of him and he has no friends. The first young girl that that twins meet is won by Aron. Cal often feels that he has no choice in his evil actions. He believes that his mother's blood that runs through his veins causes him to be bad. Most of Cal's evil actions are merely because of his desire for love and acceptance. "...everyone in the world to a large or small extent has felt rejection...and there is the story of mankind." Cal has felt this rejection throughout his entire life. He knows that Abra favors Aron so he tricks the young girl to try to win her love.

But underneath Cal's harsh appearance, is an earnest desire to live a good life. He has a genuine love for Aron and a desire to protect his weaker sibling. One night he cries and prays to God to help him be good in both his actions and thoughts. Once he gets to know his father better, Cal wants to help him recover some of the money he lost in a business venture and devotes his time to making over $20,000. Yet when he presents his gift to Adam, it is rejected and Cal feels that it is he who is being rejected. He who loves and respects his father is turned away while Aron who feels that he is almost too good to talk to his father is honored with a gold watch. This rejection causes Cal to feel that he is evil and that leading a good life is hopeless. At the end of the novel, goodness returns again to Cal. On his deathbed, Adam blesses his only living son, giving him the choice to live his life in either good or evil from that minute onward. Cal now understands that even though he has made mistakes throughout his life, his father's love will always be with him and he is free to live his life righteously.

"In uncertainty I am certain that underneath their topmost layers of frailty men want to be good and want to be loved. Indeed, most of their vices are attempted short cuts to love." Cal's attempt to lead a good life had to start with self–love and self–acceptance. Once he realized that he would make many mistakes in his life and that this was common of all of mankind, he was able to dedicate his life to living it so he will be remembered as a good person. Cal was accepted by both his father and Abra and found the love for which he had been searching for. In Cal, one can see the entire story of mankind unfold–the search for love, the feeling of rejection and hopelessness, and finally the acceptance of one's individuality. Steinbeck successfully created a story that will endure for generations because of its truth and honesty of the story of mankind and our constant battle between good and evil.

Essay: Impotency of Money in East of Eden

by Anonymous
October 21, 2003

The plot of Steinbeck's East of Eden has the issue of money tightly woven in with the stories of most of the main characters. On the surface money seems to be accepted by the society and serves as the solution to all problems; on numerous occasions, the wealthy are able to afford the best lands and latest technologies. However, a closer look reveals that money is actually quite powerless. Often Steinbeck features the affluent characters as being dispirited with their surroundings or roles in life. As a result, through his treatment of characters in East of Eden, Steinbeck suggests that financial success cannot buy happiness and love, but can only lead to isolation from society.

Many characters try to buy love, but are unsuccessful. Cyrus, for example, creates suspicion rather than admiration from his sons. "'I think he stole the money,' Charles said miserably," upon reading Cyrus's will (69). He feels betrayed by his father whom he loves. Even Adam, who never mourned Cyrus' death but instead accepted and used his share of inheritance freely, remarks "He was a thief... He stole from the G.A.R." (582). Cyrus' wealth leaves an imprint of remorse instead of respect on his sons. Charles, reciprocally, tries to purchase his father's love. He spends six bits on a knife for Cyrus' birthday, which goes unappreciated – "Where's that knife?... I never even saw him hone it" (29). Mad at the lack of attention he receives for his expensive gift, Charles tries to take out his anger on his innocent brother.

Adam does not try to get his father's attention, but instead lavishes money and attention on his wife and son Aron, where it is futile. Cathy leaves the ranch as soon as she is well enough and Aron never bothers to tell his father anything. Adam's carefully thought–out gift to Aron is not cared for, "He didn't take the gold watch" (573). Interestingly, just like the previous generation, while the father is busy chasing after the son that doesn't love him, his other, neglected son is busy finding ways to be noticed by the father. Cal works hard on a large and valuable present of fifteen thousand dollars for his father, only to have it rejected and told that it doesn't match up to his brother going to college. "I would have been so happy if you could have given me – well, what your brother has – pride in the thing he's doing, gladness in his progress. Money, even clean money, doesn't stack up with that" (544). All these unavailing attempts show that money is insufficient to purchase love.

Instead of benefits, money can actually lead to isolation. In East of Eden, the wealthy characters are often secluded from the society. Both Adam and Charles, rich from their father's will, have enough to live on comfortably so that they do not have to work and therefore interact with others. Yet Charles, even though he's rich, is such a miser that he "Never spent a dime. He pinched a dollar until the eagle screamed"

(372). He labors like crazy on the farm and never has any fun. Even little amounts gets bickered, "You remember when you sent me a telegram for a hundred dollars? You never paid it back" (108). Charles even wants to buy his brother out so that he will not be bothered (107).

His brother, Adam, also takes advantage of his financial stability by wallowing in self–pity after Cathy leaves. His wages to Lee guarantees that he and his sons will be fed and their house will be cleaned for. He never bothers to pay visits to any neighbors because since he has money, he thinks that he does not need help from them.

The Trask brothers are not the only ones separated from their surroundings because of their money. Will feels isolated in his family because of his different views on success and life. "I am the only one who ever made a dime," Will remarks proudly, trying to hide his hurt feelings of being the outsider (436). Will's greed for money is so strong that he forsakes happiness for it. "He hated Fords with a deadly hatred, but they were daily building his fortune" (364). He hates his job and never even bothers to understand the things that are making him rich: "Will Hamilton, puffing under the burden of his new fat, explained the workings of a mechanism he did not understand himself" (364). Will is the only one in his family to care about money. However, due to his feeling left out, he even speaks badly of his much–beloved father, making Adam comment in surprise, "You make Sam Hamilton sound like a criminal" (436). Will, Adam, and Charles' actions reflect that wealth is a factor that promotes isolation.

In Steinbeck's novel, the happy characters do not care much about money. Sam Hamilton is greatly loved despite his financial status, "The daughters of Samuel Hamilton were not destined to become work–destroyed farm wives. They had a pride that transcended their poverty. Samuel raised a distinctly superior breed" (147). He is constantly praised by his neighbors, to whom he is always courteous and kind. "Mr. Hamilton maybe hasn't got four bits put away, but he's our people and he's as good as we got. And he's raised the nicest family you're likely to see" (140). His achievements are not judged on his bank notes but instead on his morals, character, and family. Sam is always more concerned about changing things for the better and never gets mad at the patent firms for selling his ideas for their own profits. Steinbeck constantly quotes Sam whenever another character is thinking about the meaning of life. Even long after his death, Sam is well remembered in Lee's memory: "he had so much, he was rich. You couldn't give him anymore. Riches seem to come to the poor in spirit, the poor in interest and joy" (583). Therefore, happiness and love may be obtained by all, with no regard to materialistic values.

Money is not the solution to problems in East of Eden. It results in unhappiness as attempts to buy love fail. The wealthy also end up isolated from the society. Instead, it is the kind and generous people that end up happiest. As Lee sums up nicely, "Money's easy to make if it's money you want. But with a few exceptions people don't want money. They want luxury and they want love and they want admiration"

(541).

Quiz 1

1. **What is the novel's primary setting?**
   A. Mendicino, California
   B. Napa Valley, California
   C. Death Valley, California
   D. Salinas Valley, California

2. **Correctly pair the brothers:**
   A. Adam and Cyrus
   B. Cyrus and John
   C. Charles and Adam
   D. Cyrus and Charles

3. **The first Trask farm is located in:**
   A. Illinois
   B. New Jersey
   C. California
   D. Connecticut

4. **What crime does Cathy commit?**
   A. Murders her parents
   B. Steals a locket
   C. Steals money from a safe
   D. Murders her first lover

5. **Cathy is described by Adam as:**
   A. Angelic
   B. Red–headed
   C. Ugly
   D. Large

6. **What is Cyrus Trask's physical defect?**
   A. He is deaf
   B. He is blind
   C. He is missing an arm
   D. He has one leg

7. **Why does Charles beat Adam?**
    A. Cyrus prefers Adam's present
    B. Alice prefers Adam
    C. Adam stole his girlfriend
    D. Adam is a better shot

8. **What sort of work does Mr. Edwards do?**
    A. Runs a theatre
    B. Runs a prostitition ring
    C. Runs a casino
    D. Runs a circus

9. **While Adam is recuperating, what does Cyrus do?**
    A. Breaks his toys
    B. Enlists him in the army
    C. Infects him with the flu
    D. Buys him a ticket to Europe

10. **What present does Charles give his father?**
    A. A puppy
    B. A jacket
    C. A kitten
    D. A knife

11. **What is Mr. Edwards' initial reaction to Cathy?**
    A. He is amazed at her business acumen
    B. He is disgusted by her
    C. He falls in love with her
    D. He is scared of her

12. **Where does Mr. Edwards leave Cathy?**
    A. On his own farm
    B. On Samuel's farm
    C. On the Trask farm
    D. On his wife's farm

13. **Where does Cyrus take a job?**
    A. Illinois
    B. New Jersey
    C. California
    D. Washington D.C.

14. **Adam travels around America as:**
    A. A pilot
    B. A train porter
    C. A vagabond
    D. A chauffeur

15. **While Adam travels, what does Charles do?**
    A. Goes to prison
    B. Goes with his brother
    C. Remains in town
    D. Remains on the farm

16. **Who spends time on a chain gang?**
    A. Samuel
    B. Charles
    C. Adam
    D. Cyrus

17. **What is Lee's occupation?**
    A. Servant
    B. School teacher
    C. Shop owner
    D. Well digger

18. **Charles has a farm accident that results in:**
    A. A Broken leg
    B. A Broken arm
    C. A Scar
    D. Death

19. **What is the name of the ranch that Adam buys?**
   A. The Ruiz place
   B. The Smith place
   C. The Palms
   D. The Sanchez place

20. **Soon after her arrival in California, Cathy discovers:**
   A. She has become anemic
   B. She has the flu
   C. She is pregnant
   D. She has lost weight

21. **When Samuel comes to dinner at the Trask ranch, he leaves in a hurry because:**
   A. Adam gets drunk
   B. Lee is rude
   C. The food tastes bad
   D. Cathy fails to speak

22. **Samuel is an expert at finding:**
   A. Silver
   B. Rum
   C. Gold
   D. Water

23. **Samuel is married to:**
   A. Shirley
   B. Jane
   C. Liza
   D. Cathy

24. **How many Hamilton children are there?**
   A. Two
   B. Nine
   C. Four
   D. Seven

25. **Who sleeps with Cathy on her wedding night?**

A. Samuel
B. Charles
C. Lee
D. Adam

Quiz 1 Answer Key

1. **(D)** Salinas Valley, California
2. **(C)** Charles and Adam
3. **(D)** Connecticut
4. **(A)** Murders her parents
5. **(A)** Angelic
6. **(D)** He has one leg
7. **(A)** Cyrus prefers Adam's present
8. **(B)** Runs a prostitition ring
9. **(B)** Enlists him in the army
10. **(D)** A knife
11. **(C)** He falls in love with her
12. **(C)** On the Trask farm
13. **(D)** Washington D.C.
14. **(C)** A vagabond
15. **(D)** Remains on the farm
16. **(C)** Adam
17. **(A)** Servant
18. **(C)** A Scar
19. **(D)** The Sanchez place
20. **(C)** She is pregnant
21. **(D)** Cathy fails to speak
22. **(D)** Water
23. **(C)** Liza
24. **(B)** Nine
25. **(B)** Charles

Quiz 2

1. **The Hamilton farm is located on what kind of land?**
   A. Barren
   B. Fertile
   C. Rich
   D. Swamp

2. **What causes Samuel and Adam first to meet?**
   A. Adam needs help finding water
   B. Adam need help interpreting a Chinese manuscript
   C. Adam needs help picking apples
   D. Adam needs help building a house

3. **Describe the relationship between Cathy and Lee:**
   A. Mutual dislike
   B. Mutual love
   C. Sexual attraction
   D. Deep respect

4. **Whos acts as Cathy's midwife?**
   A. Samuel
   B. Lee
   C. Adam
   D. Liza

5. **What does Cathy do to Samuel when he attempts to comfort her?**
   A. She gets drunk with him
   B. She has sex with him
   C. She feeds him
   D. She bites him

6. **What does Adam do while Cathy gives birth?**
   A. Runs away
   B. Goes to the library
   C. Acts nervous
   D. Eats non–stop

7. **How do Lee and Samuel feel about Cathy?**
    A. They are both jealous of her
    B. They are both in love with her
    C. They are both indifferent
    D. They both think she is evil

8. **What does Cathy do to Adam before she leaves?**
    A. She shoots him
    B. She cooks him a final meal
    C. She has sex with him
    D. She tells him she loves him

9. **Cathy gives birth to:**
    A. Triplets
    B. Twin boys
    C. Twin girls
    D. A dead child

10. **After leaving Adam, Cathy lives in:**
    A. Faye's brothel
    B. The Dominican convent
    C. The Franciscan convent
    D. Lou–lou's brothel

11. **Adam responds to Cathy's departure by:**
    A. Sinking into depression
    B. Buying increased acreage
    C. Taking a second wife
    D. Traveling to Europe

12. **Faye comes to think of Cathy as:**
    A. A lover
    B. A mother
    C. A sister
    D. A daughter

13. **What does the sheriff order Cathy to do?**
    A. Buy new clothes
    B. Hire new workers
    C. Dye her hair black
    D. Buy new books

14. **What method does Kate use to kill the brothel owner?**
    A. Hammer
    B. Poison
    C. Axe
    D. Gun

15. **What happens during Faye's private party?**
    A. Cathy begins to pray
    B. They eat caviar
    C. Cathy gets drunk
    D. Faye begins to pray

16. **Why hasn't Adam named the twins?**
    A. He's waiting for their mother to name them
    B. He can't think of names
    C. He has been too depressed
    D. He hates them

17. **What biblical story do Samuel, Adam, and Lee discuss?**
    A. The Flood
    B. The Exodus
    C. Adam and Eve
    D. Cain and Abel

18. **What names does Samuel suggest for the twins?**
    A. Peter and Paul
    B. Adam and Eve
    C. Cain and Abel
    D. Joseph and Benjamin

19. **What language do the twins speak besides English?**
    A. Chinese
    B. Spanish
    C. Latin
    D. French

20. **Which of Samuel's children dies in poverty?**
    A. Dessie
    B. Una
    C. Tom
    D. Linda

21. **Who does Lee study with in San Francisco?**
    A. Two librarians and a Chinese Jesuit
    B. Four Chinese sages and a rabbi
    C. One Roman Catholic priest and a rabbi
    D. Two Orthodox priests and a Chinese sage

22. **What does the concept of timshel mean?**
    A. Thou must
    B. Perfection
    C. Absolution
    D. Thou mayest

23. **What names does Adam finally give his sons?**
    A. David and Goliath
    B. Cain and Abel
    C. Caleb and Aron
    D. Samuel and Lee

24. **Why does Samuel's last visit to the Trask ranch come about?**
    A. He is moving to Oregon
    B. He is going to live with his children
    C. He knows he is deathly ill
    D. He is going to visit China with Lee

25. **What is the secret Samuel finally tells Adam?**

A. Cathy has become a nun in Napa Valley

B. Cathy and Lee had an affair in New York

C. Adam's daughter is alive in New England

D. Cathy is living in a Salinas whorehouse

Quiz 2 Answer Key

1. **(A)** Barren
2. **(A)** Adam needs help finding water
3. **(A)** Mutual dislike
4. **(A)** Samuel
5. **(D)** She bites him
6. **(C)** Acts nervous
7. **(D)** They both think she is evil
8. **(A)** She shoots him
9. **(B)** Twin boys
10. **(A)** Faye's brothel
11. **(A)** Sinking into depression
12. **(D)** A daughter
13. **(C)** Dye her hair black
14. **(B)** Poison
15. **(C)** Cathy gets drunk
16. **(C)** He has been too depressed
17. **(D)** Cain and Abel
18. **(C)** Cain and Abel
19. **(A)** Chinese
20. **(B)** Una
21. **(B)** Four Chinese sages and a rabbi
22. **(D)** Thou mayest
23. **(C)** Caleb and Aron
24. **(B)** He is going to live with his children
25. **(D)** Cathy is living in a Salinas whorehouse

Quiz 3

1. **How does Cathy react when Adam tells her of the inheritance?**
   A. She is sad
   B. She is speechless
   C. She is suspicious
   D. She is joyful

2. **What does Cathy tell Adam when he leaves the whorehouse?**
   A. He might not the boys' father
   B. She is the boys' sister
   C. He might be her brother
   D. She is not the boys' real mother

3. **What does Adam do before he goes to see Cathy in Salinas?**
   A. He goes to the movies
   B. He joins the army
   C. He stops at a diner
   D. He attends a funeral

4. **What does Adam do after his visit to Cathy?**
   A. He goes to the movies
   B. He buys a lottery ticket
   C. He buys a car
   D. He goes to a funeral

5. **What is Lee's dearest wish?**
   A. To join the army
   B. To own a bookstore
   C. To move back to China
   D. To make love to Cathy

6. **Who needs shelter from the rain storm?**
   A. The Hamiltons
   B. The Lees
   C. The Bacons
   D. The Trasks

7. **What is the name of the eleven–year–old girl with whom Aron falls in love?**
   A. Abra
   B. Susu
   C. Adele
   D. Linda

8. **What does Aron put in the box for his new love?**
   A. A purse
   B. A rabbit
   C. Candy
   D. A snake

9. **What is written on the note Aron places in the box?**
   A. An invitation to a dance in Salinas
   B. A phone number
   C. A book list
   D. A marriage proposal

10. **What does the girl do with Aron's box?**
   A. She uses it for a doll's bed
   B. She throws it away
   C. She fills it with pencils
   D. She puts her sandwich in it

11. **How did Lee's mother die?**
   A. She was hit by a train
   B. She committed suicide by drowning
   C. She was killed in a bank hold up
   D. She was raped and murdered

12. **How much money do Adam and Cathy inherit?**
   A. $30,000
   B. $100,000
   C. $200,000
   D. $1,000,000

13. **Who does Cal overhear Adam and Lee discussing after Charles death?**
    A. His uncle
    B. His mother
    C. His sister
    D. His brother

14. **Why is Cal jealous of Aron?**
    A. Lee is smarter
    B. Aron is better looking
    C. Abra prefers Aron
    D. Cathy prefers Aron

15. **What does Liza suggest that Adam buy?**
    A. Dessie's house
    B. Her house
    C. Lee's house
    D. Tom's house

16. **What word best describes Tom Hamilton?**
    A. Depressed
    B. Dim–witted
    C. Lazy
    D. Sexy

17. **What is Tom Hamilton's primary reaction to his father's death?**
    A. He is relieved
    B. He is glad
    C. He is heartbroken
    D. He is joyful

18. **Why is Dessie Hamilton sad?**
    A. She has lost a baby
    B. She is in love with the wrong man
    C. She has a large facial scar
    D. She is barren

19. **How does Dessie die?**
   A. Her father beats her to death
   B. Her brother poisons her accidently
   C. Her sister shoots her at her request
   D. She commits suicide by drowning

20. **What does Tom do when he hears of his sister's death?**
   A. He gets married
   B. He goes to Europe
   C. He shoots himself
   D. He buys a new farm with the inheritance

21. **What does Lee do after he moves to San Francisco?**
   A. He goes to China
   B. He gets married
   C. He comes back home
   D. He commits suicide

22. **What does Abra do to Aron after he starts school?**
   A. She kisses him
   B. She gets him expelled
   C. She throws books at him
   D. She kicks him

23. **What purchase does Lee make for the Trask kitchen?**
   A. An icebox
   B. A new couch
   C. A telephone
   D. A chandelier

24. **After Abra hears rumours, what advice does she give Aron?**
   A. To find out about his father
   B. To find out about his mother
   C. To find out about his brother
   D. To find out about his dead uncle

25. **What sort of work does Will Hamilton do?**

A. He is a businessman

B. He is a doctor

C. He is a lawyer

D. He is a veterinarian

Quiz 3 Answer Key

1. **(C)** She is suspicious
2. **(A)** He might not the boys' father
3. **(D)** He attends a funeral
4. **(C)** He buys a car
5. **(B)** To own a bookstore
6. **(C)** The Bacons
7. **(A)** Abra
8. **(B)** A rabbit
9. **(D)** A marriage proposal
10. **(B)** She throws it away
11. **(D)** She was raped and murdered
12. **(B)** $100,000
13. **(B)** His mother
14. **(C)** Abra prefers Aron
15. **(A)** Dessie's house
16. **(A)** Depressed
17. **(C)** He is heartbroken
18. **(B)** She is in love with the wrong man
19. **(B)** Her brother poisons her accidently
20. **(C)** He shoots himself
21. **(C)** He comes back home
22. **(A)** She kisses him
23. **(A)** An icebox
24. **(B)** To find out about his mother
25. **(A)** He is a businessman

Quiz 4

1. **What name does Cathy take after leaving Adam?**
   A. Dessie
   B. Kate
   C. Wilma
   D. Kathy

2. **What is the name of the drunk who brings Cal to the brothel?**
   A. Rabbit Holman
   B. Squirrel Martin
   C. Road–Kill Kelleher
   D. John Murphy

3. **Who comes to bail Cal out of jail?**
   A. His father
   B. His mother
   C. His sister
   D. His brother

4. **What is the name of Kate's stalker?**
   A. Cal
   B. Joe
   C. Adam
   D. Aron

5. **After Cal tells his father he knows about his mother, what do they decide to do?**
   A. Tell Lee
   B. Keep the knowledge from Aron
   C. Tell Aron
   D. Tell the sheriff

6. **What is Ethyl's occupation?**
   A. Doctor
   B. Maid
   C. Cook
   D. Prostitute

7. **Why does Aron want to leave home?**
   A. He wants to elope with Cathy
   B. He's ashamed his brother got a girl pregnant
   C. He's ashamed of his father's financial losses
   D. He wants to go to Harvard

8. **How does Cal plan on making his father love him?**
   A. By marrying Abra
   B. By becoming friends with Charles
   C. By earning money to replace his father's losses
   D. By going to Stanford

9. **On what holiday does Cal present his gift to Adam?**
   A. Easter
   B. Thanksgiving
   C. St. Patrick's Day
   D. Christmas

10. **How much money does Lee lend Cal?**
   A. $2
   B. $1,000
   C. $5,000
   D. $100,000

11. **What is the name of Kate's bodyguard?**
   A. Rabbitt Holman
   B. Rupert Mandrake
   C. Joe Valery
   D. Horace Quinn

12. **What word best describes Aron's state of mind upon returning home from college?**
   A. Joyful
   B. Inspired
   C. Miserable
   D. Ambitious

13. **How does Adam react to Cal's gift?**
    A. He angrily rejects it
    B. He burns it
    C. He slaps Cal
    D. He loves it and says he will cherish it forever

14. **Where does the jealous Cal take his brother to meet their mother?**
    A. A brothel
    B. A juke joint
    C. The library
    D. A coffee shop

15. **Who does Kate contact before comitting suicide?**
    A. The doctor
    B. The sheriff
    C. The druggist
    D. The minister

16. **What is the name of the book Kate thinks about after taking the poison?**
    A. Tess of the D'urbervilles
    B. War and Peace
    C. Pride and Prejudice
    D. Alice in Wonderland

17. **How does Joe Valery die?**
    A. The sheriff shoots him
    B. The minister stabs him
    C. The doctor poisons him
    D. He falls off his horse and hits his head

18. **How does Cal respond when questioned about Aron's whereabouts?**
    A. "Am I my brother's keeper?"
    B. "Am I supposed to look after him?"
    C. "How should I know?"
    D. "It's not my business"

19. **To whom does Lee give his mother's jade ornament?**
    A. Abra
    B. Cathy
    C. Olive
    D. Ethyl

20. **Who does Kate designate as her sole beneficiary?**
    A. Charles
    B. Cal
    C. Adam
    D. Aron

21. **What does the telegram that Lee receives tell him?**
    A. That Kate is dead
    B. That Aron is dead
    C. That Lee's mother is dead
    D. That Adam has inherited $100,000

22. **What does Abra give to Lee?**
    A. A new pan
    B. A cookbook
    C. A rose
    D. A kiss

23. **After Adam's stroke, who does Lee tell Cal to find?**
    A. God
    B. Adam
    C. Abra
    D. Aron

24. **Who stands around Adam's deathbed?**
    A. Cal, Abra and Lee
    B. Kate, Cathy and Lee
    C. Cal, Aron and Cathy
    D. Cyrus, Abra and Lee

25. **What is the final word of the novel?**

A. Timshel

B. God

C. Amen

D. Mahema

Quiz 4 Answer Key

1. (**B**) Kate
2. (**A**) Rabbit Holman
3. (**A**) His father
4. (**A**) Cal
5. (**B**) Keep the knowledge from Aron
6. (**D**) Prostitute
7. (**C**) He's ashamed of his father's financial losses
8. (**C**) By earning money to replace his father's losses
9. (**B**) Thanksgiving
10. (**C**) $5,000
11. (**C**) Joe Valery
12. (**C**) Miserable
13. (**A**) He angrily rejects it
14. (**A**) A brothel
15. (**B**) The sheriff
16. (**D**) Alice in Wonderland
17. (**A**) The sheriff shoots him
18. (**B**) "Am I supposed to look after him?"
19. (**A**) Abra
20. (**D**) Aron
21. (**B**) That Aron is dead
22. (**D**) A kiss
23. (**C**) Abra
24. (**A**) Cal, Abra and Lee
25. (**A**) Timshel

Made in the USA
Lexington, KY
07 August 2011